QUEEN'S
IN THEIR NAME

Photographed by
Julian Calder

Text written, compiled and edited by
Tamsin Shelton

Foreword by
Alastair Bruce

JCP

Front cover: A detail of the richly embroidered banner that hangs from the instruments of State trumpeters. The lion and the unicorn of the royal coat of arms represent England and Scotland respectively, surmounted by the royal crown. The garter bearing the motto Honi soit qui mal y pense ('Evil to him who evil thinks') symbolises the Order of the Garter, the most ancient and most senior Order of Chivalry, of which The Queen is Sovereign. The motto of the Sovereign, Dieu et mon droit, means 'God and my right'. Pure silk damask is used for the banner as it acts as a strong base for the heavy embroidery and resists gathering. Humphries Weaving, based in the traditional silk-weaving town of Sudbury, Suffolk, has supplied these special fabrics since its foundation in 1972.

Back cover: The Queen's Keys, held here by a Yeoman Warder of the Tower of London, play a central role in the Ceremony of the Keys, dating back to the mid-1300s in the reign of Edward III, when the outer gates of the fortress are locked at 10 p.m. by the Chief Yeoman Warder. Dressed in the traditional red Watch Coat and Tudor bonnet, he carries a lantern in one hand, lit with a single candle, and The Queen's Keys in the other. He leaves the Byward Tower at exactly 9.53 p.m. and walks to the archway of the Bloody Tower, where he is met by an escort from the Tower's military garrison. They all march to the outer gates where the Chief and the Watchman close and lock the gates and do the same with the gates of the Middle and Byward Towers. At the end of the ceremony, the Chief Yeoman Warder raises his bonnet high and declares, 'God preserve Queen Elizabeth,' to which the guard answers 'Amen' as the clock strikes 10 and 'The Last Post' is played on the bugle. To complete the ancient ritual for another night, the Chief Yeoman Warder takes the keys back to The Queen's House to return them to The Queen's representative at the Tower, the Resident Governor.

Half title: The Sovereign sits beside the Symbols of Sovereignty in the Throne Room at Buckingham Palace. The Imperial State Crown has a sapphire in the top cross, which came from Edward the Confessor's ring; below it hang Elizabeth I's pearl earrings. The massive balas ruby, owned by the Black Prince and worn by Henry V at Agincourt, sits above the bright Second Star of Africa diamond. The Sword of State was traditionally the monarch's personal weapon and is the symbol of both her authority and power. The throne, with the Royal Cypher, was used when The Queen made her Oath during the Coronation in 1953.

Frontispiece: The brooch of The Queen's Chaplain is pinned to the left breast of the cassock. The Clerk of the Closet has his own badge of office which is worn on a ribbon around his neck.

Overleaf: The wild landscape of the Scottish Highlands is where the culture and traditions of Scotland's Clan system developed. Here the Chief of the Chiefs, Queen Elizabeth II, stands by the Gelder Burn on the Balmoral Estate, wearing her mantle as Sovereign of the Most Ancient and Most Noble Order of the Thistle. Although Queen of the United Kingdom, she is increasingly accorded the ancient title of her ancestors, as Queen of Scots. From her shoulders and held by white satin ties hangs the Collar of the Order, which is a chain of alternate golden thistles and rue sprigs, plants that abound in this terrain. From it is suspended the Jewel, showing Scotland's patron saint and his saltire cross. The star of the Order is also based on St Andrew's Cross, which legend says appeared in a vision to the Scots and Picts before they defeated the West Saxons.

INTRODUCTION

When Prince George was born in 2013, becoming third in line to the throne, it occurred to me that, in due course if he had a son, we would not hear many of the titles with 'Queen's' in their name for at least 100 years. A few will remain 'Queen's' as they are specifically named after Elizabeth I, such as the Westminster School Scholars; Queen's Nurses are named after Queen Victoria while, conversely, there will always be King's Scholars at Eton (named after Henry VII) and The King's Troop Royal Horse Artillery is named after George VI. But upon the accession of Prince George's grandfather, the Prince of Wales, most of the titles in this book will become 'King's' until the line of succession passes once again to a female. ¶ I set out, therefore, to photograph a range of titles, offices and objects that bear 'Queen's' in their name. I acknowledge that this is not a comprehensive list but it gives an idea of the variety of titles and the people who bear them. My aim was to capture not just the individual or object with that title but the position itself. It was important to me to include in the portrait living details such as the location, the uniform, a symbol, an action and, if possible, the history associated with each position, as visualising history has been a lifelong interest of mine. A picture for a book like this should contain as much relevant information as possible, not yielding all its secrets at first glance but making the viewer look and return to look again and again. It is not an ephemeral newspaper or magazine image, but an enduring record of ordinary people doing extraordinary things as part of our shared national history. ¶ A camera is bound to take a likeness, but I strive to take a portrait that is more than that, which reveals more than a subject's face. Often I have to achieve this in no more than 40 minutes, unlike a painter who may have as long as 40 hours. Before I set out to take a portrait, I have a vague idea of what I am looking for – a picture in my mind's eye. Ideally, I try to visit the location, and for these portraits I had a discussion with the subjects beforehand in order to get to know them a little and to share my ideas so we would feel at ease with each other. All the subjects are looking directly at me, as I wanted there to be a relationship reflecting the fact that we made the portrait together. Indeed, many of the images in this book came from the last 15 frames when that all-important bond had been formed between photographer and subject. ¶ This project has taken four years to complete, hampered by the various lockdowns caused by the Covid-19 pandemic. Some of the people featured here have moved to other jobs, have retired or, as is the case with the Surveyor of The Queen's Pictures and the Surveyor of The Queen's Works of Art, their roles have ceased to exist. My thanks to everyone who agreed to be photographed, taking time and trouble to share my vision, and also to the members of various organisations that arranged for the pictures to be taken. ¶ My grateful thanks to Her Majesty The Queen for giving her consent for me to photograph members of the Royal Household for this project. It has been both a pleasure and a privilege to take all the portraits in this book.

Julian Calder

FOREWORD

Julian Calder and I have been seeking ways to bring the hidden narrative of the United Kingdom's treasure of appointments and traditions to life, through image and text, for nearly 40 years. In his latest book, Julian has followed that inspiration forwards by seeking out and recording many of the posts and objects that have 'Queen's' as a dedicative part of their name. ¶ With each, he has applied the same courteous, clear and single-minded discipline that is the leitmotiv of his art; much as he displayed when we led Her Majesty into the middle of a Balmoral moor in order to capture her own pivotal headship of all. ¶ 'Please may I take command?' was how Julian started the photo shoot with The Queen. With a very practical 'Yes, do', Her Majesty proceeded to comply with Julian's bidding and was content to turn her head, lift her chin, move the mantle of the Order of the Thistle, or do whatever the photographer required. ¶ At the end, with equal charm, Julian stepped forward and relinquished 'command', and the bejewelled monarch returned to the mud-spattered Land Rover. Her train of bottle green velvet, lined with white taffeta, was bundled in after her and the vehicle splashed and bumped along the rough track, just as the rain began to fall once more. ¶ Julian and I had secured an image that few believed possible. We had been supported by Angela Kelly (The Queen's Dresser) and Paul Whybrew (The Queen's Page of the Backstairs). Many did not believe it to be real. It had required enormous planning, not least to include persuading the Sovereign to dress in both robes and tiara during her annual holiday and drive nearly half an hour along puddled tracks into the Aberdonian wilderness, on a day that only a few hours before had seen Biblical stair-rod rain. ¶ This is but one example of the ingenuity, preparation, conviction and care that Julian applies to every portrait gathered together in this book. They encompass a spectrum of extant appointments that are, through their name, dedicated to supporting The Queen in her life as Sovereign. ¶ Julian, like me, has a passion for bringing what is often derided as 'flummery' out of misunderstanding and back into the reach of all, by anchoring it firmly in the provenance of its historic purpose and utility. Each portrait tells a story that is mostly founded in utility. Some echo an ancient tradition, but all of them make up a collection unlike any other in the world. ¶ They reach effortlessly into the times when each national strand of the United Kingdom's constituent nations took form. In the case of England, William the Conqueror had made everything his own by right of conquest in 1066. The feudal construct he imposed and the legal framework in which it sat may have been ruptured when the Barons held Richard II to his signature on Magna Carta, but kingship evolved to the present as each monarch shaped their own pragmatism. ¶ The Scottish story differed because chiefship, rather than overlordship, shaped the nation. Kings and Queens of Scots, including my infamous forebear Robert the Bruce, held leadership over the people, not their land, and The Queen's links to titles in Scotland still reflect this subtlety. ¶ In 1689, England's Parliament, which had shared the Scottish monarch since Elizabeth I died without an heir in 1603, became sovereign and chose its king, thus altering the very nature of kingship. But, in the quasi-republican construct that emerged then and still survives today, space was always left for the magic of monarchy to embody power and bring its apolitical continuity to affairs. That continuity of reigns and the utilitarian needs of four centuries of court life have nurtured the appointments you will see in these pages. ¶ Sometimes their titles seem humorous but, before you smile, read. What now sounds exceptional or strange was once entirely understood as ordinary. Julian selects his subjects and takes each into the normality of their history in order to visualise that provenance, in the context of both the present and of The Queen they serve.

Alastair Bruce

QUEEN'S CONSORT

In 2009, at the age of 88, The Duke of Edinburgh overtook Queen Charlotte, wife of George III, as the longest serving British Consort. Since Queen Elizabeth's accession on 6 February 1952, he had spent 57 years as companion to the Sovereign. While, constitutionally, the wives of ruling Kings currently become Queen Consorts, the husbands of female monarchs have no right to an equivalent title. He was therefore titled neither Prince Consort nor King Consort, but was raised to the peerage as Duke of Edinburgh, Earl of Merioneth and Baron Greenwich in 1947 upon his marriage to Princess Elizabeth and became a Prince of the United Kingdom in 1957. ¶ Neither of the Duke's two predecessors since the Union of the Kingdoms of England and Scotland in 1707 were considered King Consort. Prince George of Denmark, husband of Queen Anne, was raised to the peerage of England as the Duke of Cumberland in 1689, several years before his wife's accession in 1702. Prince Albert of Saxe-Coburg and Gotha, husband of Queen Victoria, was the only male Consort to have officially held the title of Prince Consort, after he was granted it in 1857. ¶ In his role as Consort, The Duke of Edinburgh was by The Queen's side at countless events across the United Kingdom and the world, and had also completed 22,219 solo engagements since 1952 until his retirement from public engagements in 2017. At a luncheon at Banqueting House given to celebrate their Golden Wedding anniversary in 1997, The Queen paid tribute to the Duke's steadfastness as her Consort, saying: 'he has, quite simply, been my strength and stay all these years, and I, and his whole family, in this and in many other countries, owe him a debt greater than he would ever claim or we shall ever know.'

The Queen wears the State Dress, Robe of State and Imperial State Crown, as worn for the State Opening of Parliament. Prince Philip's uniform of the Admiral of the Fleet bears a selection of medals, many earned during his time as a Naval officer in the Second World War. The Duke saw action in the Battle of Crete; he helped protect convoys of Australian soldiers sailing across the Indian Ocean and was present in Tokyo Bay when Japan surrendered. Other medals represent his long years of service as The Duke of Edinburgh.

Camera Press Ranald Mackechnie

This image captures a rare moment in British history, when three lines of succession are portrayed with the reigning Sovereign. These four generations of the Royal Family trace a line of inheritance through the 20th and 21st centuries, from 1926 when Princess Elizabeth was born to the then Duke and Duchess of York, to 2013 and the birth of Prince George, first son of the Duke and Duchess of Cambridge, and grandson of Prince Charles, the Prince of Wales, and the late Diana, Princess of Wales. ¶ Taken in the Throne Room of Buckingham Palace, the photograph was released in January 2020 to mark the start of a new decade, four years after a similar, albeit seated, image of the heirs and their Sovereign was issued to celebrate The Queen's 90th birthday. That earlier image was used on a set of Royal Mail stamps. ¶ The very first official photograph of the four generations was taken in Clarence House on the occasion of Prince George's christening in October 2013 as part of the formal christening photographs. This echoed an historic image released almost 120 years earlier of Queen Victoria and her three heirs at the christening of her great-grandson Prince Edward of York, the future King Edward VIII,

Getty Images

in 1894. That picture, taken in the former royal residence of the White Lodge, Richmond Park, also showed the future kings George V and Edward VII.

Five years after Queen Victoria's great-grandson, Prince Edward of York, was christened, The Queen's Heirs gathered for another formal portrait. This time they were photographed at Osborne House on the Isle of Wight, in August 1899, shortly after Victoria's 80th birthday. The photographer was John Chancellor, who had a studio in Dublin from the 1860s and was a popular choice for society portraits. Standing behind Victoria are her grandson Prince George, Duke of York, and her son Edward, Prince of Wales. The four monarchs would rule for a total of 99 years, although King Edward VIII abdicated five months before he was due to be crowned. In a letter to her daughter Princess Victoria in June 1894 about the birth of Prince Edward of York, Queen Victoria wrote that 'it seems that it has never happened in this Country that there should be three direct Heirs as well as the Sovereign alive'.

QUEEN'S DRESSER

Among the Royal Household, perhaps the person who has the closest daily contact with The Queen is the holder of the title Personal Advisor, Curator and Senior Dresser to Her Majesty The Queen (Jewellery, Insignias and Wardrobe) – more commonly referred to as The Queen's Dresser. With responsibility for designing, curating and maintaining the sovereign's wardrobe, the Dresser is one of the few non-family members who is allowed to touch The Queen, essential when fitting a new outfit or assisting Her Majesty to dress for a state ceremony. ¶ The current Dresser, Angela Kelly, has worked in the Royal Household since 1994 and has held the post since 2002. While Mrs Kelly was not formally trained in dressmaking, she has designed some of The Queen's most memorable outfits, including the pale yellow dress and coat she wore to the wedding of the Duke and Duchess of Cambridge in 2011 and the crystal and lace peach beaded cocktail dress worn for the Opening Ceremony of the London Olympics in 2012. ¶ Fabrics must be carefully tested to make sure they will not crease, and the Dresser and her team frequently source fabrics from the Buckingham Palace stockroom, some of which have been kept since the 1960s. Colour choice is important to ensure that The Queen can be visible in crowds or from a distance; the white dress worn for the Diamond Jubilee River Pageant in 2012, for example, was designed to contrast with the deep red seats of the Royal Barge Gloriana. The Queen is attuned to sartorial symbolism, and the Dresser often incorporates appropriate emblems into a new outfit. When, in 2011, The Queen made the first visit to the Republic of Ireland by a reigning British monarch in 100 years, her white silk evening gown for the state banquet was hand-sewn with over 2,000 silk shamrocks, symbolic of Ireland. ¶ While setting trends does not dictate The Queen's choice of clothing, a delicate balance must be struck between formality and approachability, tradition and modernity. Following Her Majesty's 90th birthday celebrations, Angela Kelly raised the idea of an award to honour an emerging British fashion designer. The Queen Elizabeth II Award for British Design was inaugurated in 2018 by the British Fashion Council, and deepens the link between fashion and the monarch that has marked the reign of Queen Elizabeth.

Overleaf: The Queen's Dresser stands with some of Her Majesty's ceremonial robes. The mantle of the Sovereign of the Most Ancient and Most Noble Order of the Thistle (left) is worn for the service at the Chapel of the Order of the Thistle in St Giles' Cathedral, Edinburgh, when The Queen installs new Members. The Queen travels to the State Opening of Parliament wearing the George IV State Diadem (centre), set with 1,333 diamonds, before donning the crimson velvet Robe of State and the Imperial State Crown. The mantle of the Most Noble Order of the Garter (right) is worn on Garter Day every June, for the investiture in the Throne Room at Windsor Castle and the grand procession to a service in St George's Chapel.

Inspiration for one of the outfits worn by The Queen during her visit to Northern Ireland during her 2012 Diamond Jubilee Tour came from the corridors of Windsor Castle. The Queen's Dresser had already chosen a pale blue material when she was struck by its similarity to the shade of china in the Castle's Wedgwood collection. She added the lace detailing inspired by the delicate decoration on some of the Wedgwood pieces. The Queen wore the outfit again in 2014 at the Household Cavalry Standards Parade, at which she presented the new Standards.

QUEEN'S PAGES OF THE BACKSTAIRS

The Pages of the Backstairs, or Pages of the Presence, are four senior servants of the Royal Household who personally attend the Sovereign and their spouse. First appointed by Queen Anne in the 1700s, the Page of the Backstairs was created to distinguish between the Ladies of the Bedchamber as Queen Anne's closest male servant. The control of access dates back to the era when the Page positioned himself, literally, at the bottom of the 'Back' or 'Privy' stairs, which led to the Sovereign's private rooms. So important was his role, the Page was set apart from the other domestic staff of the Royal Household and was paid an annual salary of over £100, rising to £400 under Queen Victoria. ¶ Today, they are the only individuals who can grant members of the Royal Household access to The Queen's private apartments, and are personally chosen by Her Majesty for their qualities of loyalty and discretion. The Pages' office is situated next to The Queen's lift, at the entrance to her private apartments. One is in her presence at all times, serving her drinks and meals, delivering the red boxes that contain confidential papers dispatched to Her Majesty from her Private Secretary several times a day, and dealing with all of her domestic arrangements, including the care of the corgis. The Pages of the Backstairs even attend The Queen in her private time on holiday, or with friends and family. ¶ When important visitors such as ambassadors, heads of state and other dignitaries come to see The Queen, they are personally met by a Page of the Backstairs, who will then escort them to Her Majesty. At state functions, they stand immediately behind The Queen's chair, and when she is travelling in a state coach they will be standing at the back of the carriage.

Standing on the Equerries' Entrance Staircase at Windsor Castle, one of The Queen's Pages of the Backstairs holds the sword with which Her Majesty bestows knighthoods at investitures. The sword belonged to her father, George VI, and was worn by him as Colonel of the Scots Guards. With his day livery, the Page is wearing a Balmoral tartan waistcoat, a gift to the Pages by The Queen in 2012, her Diamond Jubilee year. This is a particular honour, as Balmoral tartan can only be worn with express permission of the Sovereign. The other Page of the Backstairs is carrying a red box stamped with the Royal Cypher, a crown and the words 'The Queen'. He wears white tie, which is worn for official and State occasions. Both Pages are wearing their miniature medals awarded in recognition of long years of faithful and discreet service to Her Majesty. On State occasions the full size medals are worn.

QUEEN'S STUD GROOM

The Queen's love for and knowledge of horses is legendary, a passion nurtured since her first riding lesson at the age of three and the gift of her first pony, Peggy, by her grandfather King George V on her fourth birthday. Horses play a central role in State Ceremonial, from the Windsor greys that pull the State Coach that takes the Sovereign to the State Opening of Parliament, to the 250 military horses that take part in the annual Queen's Birthday Parade. Yet in private moments, The Queen still seeks the company of her own ponies and horses and can be seen riding in Windsor Great Park on one of her beloved black fell ponies, always accompanied by her Stud Groom. ¶ The Queen's Stud Groom is based at Windsor's Royal Mews with responsibility for the royal horses stabled there and the Riding School. The Mews were built in 1841 and today hold around 90 horses, as well as staff accommodation and the State carriages, coaches and cars used by The Queen and members of the Royal Family during State occasions. ¶ The current Queen's Stud Groom is a former Riding Master with the Household Cavalry, and since assuming the role 24 years ago, he has taught all The Queen's grandchildren to ride. Any member of the Royal Household may learn to ride at the School too, if they wish. ¶ Some of the Royal Family's favourite horses are buried in the grounds of the Mews, including Burmese, The Queen's Trooping horse for 18 years, Sanction, Her Majesty's favourite riding horse, Doublet, the Princess Royal's European three-day eventer, and Polly Perkins, one of The Duke of Edinburgh's driving ponies.

The Queen's Stud Groom rides George, given to the Prince of Wales by the Royal Canadian Mounted Police, at Windsor Castle. He holds the tethers of Muthwaite Dawn Chorus (left) and Emma (right), two of The Queen's black fell ponies. The Queen has owned and ridden this ancient hardy breed all her life and is the Patron of the Fell Pony Society. To celebrate Her Majesty's 90th birthday in 2016, 128 fell ponies and riders formed a guard of honour at Windsor Castle, as The Queen drove past in a carriage pulled by four fell ponies.

QUEEN'S EQUERRIES

The post of Equerry has existed for centuries, held originally by squires working for persons of high rank. One duty was to tether their master's horse with a piece of rope carried on their shoulder, which is thought to be the origin of the aiguillettes worn on the right shoulder. All Equerries were originally called 'Equerries of the Crown Stable' ('equerry' is an Anglicisation of the French *écurie*, meaning 'stable'), and duties included breaking in and preparing the monarch's horses and riding in attendance upon the Sovereign. Court pronunciation stresses the second syllable, supported by the French derivation of the word. ¶ Today, The Queen's Equerries are among her most trusted attendants, seen at her side assisting with official engagements and welcoming notable guests. The appointment took on a special importance following The Duke of Edinburgh's retirement from public engagements in 2017. ¶ Of The Queen's three Equerries, the senior and permanent one is designated Deputy Master of the Household and Equerry. The Junior Equerry, appointed from each of the three branches of the Armed Forces in turn, holds office for three years. Both work closely with the Private Secretaries, Master of the Household, Comptroller, Lord Chamberlain's Office and the Households of other Royal Family members. ¶ The third Equerry is known as an Assistant Equerry and is appointed from the Coldstream Guards. This post was created unofficially when Lieutenant-Colonel Sir Eric Penn was the Comptroller of the Royal Household from 1964 to 1981. Prior to that there had been three full time Equerries at the Palace, one from each Service. It then dropped to just one full time Service Equerry, until, inevitably, the Palace found that at busy times one wasn't enough. So the Regimental Headquarters of the various Guards Regiments stepped in on an unofficial part-time basis. After a while the Palace found it simpler to deal with just one Regiment and the Assistant Equerry was given to the Coldstream Guards, the only Foot Guards Regiment without a Royal Colonel. ¶ Equerries are also appointed from the three Services to certain members of the Royal Family. The Duke of Edinburgh relinquished his service Equerry to enable his grandson the Duke of Cambridge to have one, yet retained his two Assistant Equerries, Captains from the Royal Marines and the Grenadier Guards.

The Queen's Equerries stand before Philip Jackson's 2003 statue of Queen Elizabeth II at the end of Queen Anne's Walk, Windsor Great Park. The aiguillettes are worn on the right shoulder for an officer appointed to a Member of the Royal Family, unlike a member of the military staff who wear theirs on the left shoulder.

QUEEN'S PIPER

'We have heard nothing but bagpipes since we have been in the beautiful Highlands & I have become so fond of it that I mean to have a piper,' wrote Queen Victoria to her mother during her first visit to Scotland in 1842. Victoria enlisted the help of her host in the Highlands, the Marquess of Breadalbane, to recruit a royal piper. The first holder of the post was Angus Mackay, a noted composer of pipe music. While she was in residence at Balmoral Victoria required him to play every weekday at 9 a.m. beneath her window, as well as at balls and special occasions including during the erection of a cairn in 1852 to commemorate The Queen's purchase of the Balmoral Estate. ¶ When Mackay retired in 1854 the Army provided his replacement, Pipe Major William Ross of the Black Watch, beginning a custom that has been followed ever since. The current Queen's Piper is the 16th holder of the post, all Pipe Majors serving in Scottish, and in one case Irish, regiments. The Queen's Piper retains his army status and pay while on secondment to the Royal Household, and the position is one of the highest accolades available to a piper serving in the Armed Forces. He still plays every morning outside The Queen's window when she is in residence at Buckingham Palace, Windsor Castle, the Palace of Holyroodhouse or Balmoral Castle, but he is also responsible for co-ordinating the dozen British Army pipers who play at State banquets. ¶ The Piper becomes an Honorary Page of the Presence at events such as investitures, garden parties and receptions, escorting The Queen to various audiences throughout the day and supervising the arrival and departure of Ambassadors and other guests. This dual role demands as much tact and discretion as it does musical ability. During the Balmoral season, which lasts approximately 12 weeks, it is also the Piper's responsibility to teach members of the Royal Household the Scottish reels for the Ghillies' Ball, which he organises on behalf of The Queen. ¶ As Pipers perform without music, The Queen's Piper must be able to carry hundreds of tunes in his head to provide variety for the daily piping. Indeed, Gordon Webster, who was a Pipe Major in the Scots Guards before becoming The Queen's Piper between 1995 and 1998, noted that Her Majesty 'didn't like that you repeated tunes every other day, so I probably had about 700 or 800 tunes under my belt'.

Previous page: Standing by Loch Muick on the Balmoral Estate, The Queen's Piper wears the Balmoral tartan, designed by Queen Victoria and Prince Albert in grey and red and worn only on the estate; elsewhere the Piper wears the green Hunting Stewart in the morning and the red Royal Stewart for evening duties. The Prince Charlie jacket is high cut at the waist with long button-adorned flaps at the back and three large silver buttons on the lower sections of the sleeves. The Balmoral bonnet bears two feathers, and the bass drone of the pipes carries the Sovereign's Piping Banner. By tradition, in the top of his right sock the Piper wears the *sgian dubh* (a small knife) belonging to John Brown, Queen Victoria's trusted Highland servant.

Royal Collection

This watercolour portrait by William Wyld shows Angus Mackay, the first Queen's Piper, playing the bagpipes at Balmoral in 1852. It is part of an album compiled by Albert Edward, Prince of Wales, later Edward VII, which is in the Royal Collection.

THE NEAREST GUARD 1509-2009

QUEEN'S BODY GUARD OF THE HONOURABLE CORPS OF GENTLEMEN-AT-ARMS

Henry VIII was keen to protect his royal person when he took the throne in 1509, and soon established a close body guard of 50 young nobles, armed with spears and lances. This 'new and sumptuous Troop of Gentlemen' were known as the Band of Gentlemen Pensioners, a title that showed that the King paid for their pension, or board and lodging. ¶ Before long this new Band of well-trained fighting men was put to the test. In June 1513 Henry landed at Calais with his army and the Band of Gentlemen, commanded by their first Captain, the Earl of Essex, to challenge Louis XII in the Battle of the Spurs. The Band numbered 400 mounted men for this invasion, and a Standard Bearer was appointed in preparation for war, together with a Harbinger, who kept the Men-at-Arms victualled with lodgings, and a Clerk of the Cheque, who checked that all were present and paid. ¶ The last time they served as a military body guard was for Charles I in the Civil War. At the Battle of Edgehill in 1642 they played a crucial role when they protected the 12-year-old Prince of Wales and his 11-year-old brother James, the future King James II and VI, ushering them from the bloody field of action when the King's centre gave way. After the Interregnum Charles II restored the Band as a ceremonial guard of retired officers of merit, and it was renamed the Honourable Corps of Gentlemen-at-Arms by William IV. Now, it is the Corps that stands closest to The Queen on important occasions such as visits by Heads of State, the Garter service at Windsor Castle and the State Opening of Parliament. The Gentlemen-at-Arms also attend garden parties, where they form the lanes through which the members of the Royal Family walk. The Corps' final act of duty in the Sovereign's reign is to make up one of the four-man detachments that guard the Sovereign's catafalque during the lying-in-state in Westminster Hall. ¶ The Honourable Corps consists of 27 Gentlemen and five Officers: Captain, Lieutenant, Standard Bearer, Clerk of the Cheque and Harbinger. All are ex-military officers, bar the Captain, who is always the Government Chief Whip in the House of Lords. The uniform is that of a Dragoon Guard's officer from the 1840s, with epaulettes to protect against sword blows and gilt-metal helmets adorned with 18-inch swan plumes. Officers wear cavalry swords and carry sticks of office, which they receive from the Sovereign on appointment. ¶ When the Corps celebrated its 500th anniversary in 2009 The Queen presented a special riband to be displayed on the Standard and paid tribute with these words: 'The evils against which the Sovereign required protection in 1509 have, I expect, changed a little over the years but the loyalty of the Body Guard remains undimmed.'

Previous page: The Queen's Body Guard rally round the Standard Bearer in Colour Court, St James's Palace. The Standard is adorned with the riband presented by The Queen to her 'Nearest Guard'.

Members of the Honourable Corps of Gentlemen-at-Arms flank the Comptroller of the Lord Chamberlain's Office, who bears the Imperial State Crown from the House of Lords after the State Opening of Parliament. The Earl Marshall, the 18th Duke of Norfolk, bows to the Crown, the symbol of Sovereignty, while holding the Field Marshall's baton.

ENGINE COURT

QUEEN'S BODY GUARD OF THE YEOMEN OF THE GUARD

The Queen's Body Guard of the Yeomen of the Guard is the most ancient royal guard and military corps in Britain. It traces its formation to the Battle of Bosworth in 1485 at which Henry Tudor, Earl of Richmond, defeated Richard III to become England's first Tudor king. Henry's victory divided the country, so, following the example of the French king who employed the Scottish Guard to ensure his security, Henry formed 50 of his loyal archers into a company called the Yeomen of the Guard of Our Lord the King to protect him. ¶ It is said that Henry chose his Guard from the yeomen of England not only because he believed they were the true heart of the nation, but also because he did not trust the nobility, who were known to stoop to plots and tricks to advance themselves. So closely were they trusted, Charles II took his Guard with him into exile, giving the Body Guard an unbroken history of over 530 years of royal service. ¶ Today all members, except the Captain, are retired from the Armed Services. The Captain is a political appointment (the Government's Deputy Chief Whip in the House of Lords) but the Commanding Officer, or Lieutenant, the Adjutant and Clerk of the Cheque (same appointment), the two Exons and the Ensign are retired army officers. The other ranks comprise the Messenger Sergeant Major and Wardrobe Keeper (same appointment), the Second Messenger Sergeant Major, the three Divisional Sergeant Majors and the 54 Yeomen; all must have retired from the Navy, the Royal Marines, the Army or the Royal Air Force at the minimum rank of Sergeant. Most importantly, they must have been awarded the Long Service and Good Conduct Medal. ¶ The appointments of Yeoman Bed Goer and Yeomen Bed Hanger are believed to date back to Tudor times when the Bed Goers escorted the monarch to the royal bedchamber, preceded by the Bed Hangers who went ahead to ensure that no one ill-intentioned lurked therein. There is evidence that the Yeomen Bed Hangers were required to 'roll on the bed and pearce the bedding and hangings with their blades' to ensure the monarch's safety. ¶ The Body Guard's first ceremonial duty of the year is the Epiphany Service at the Chapel Royal in St James's Palace, when they escort the gold, frankincense and myrrh to the altar. The Guard escorts The Queen at all State occasions, such as garden parties, investitures, State visits and banquets, the State Opening of Parliament and Orders of Chivalry services.

Previous page: The Queen's Body Guard of the Yeomen of the Guard are still armed with a partisan, a tall spear-like weapon remarkably similar in design to that used in the early 1500s. Today's uniform is almost identical to that of the Yeomen Warders who guard the Tower of London. The Yeomen of the Guard can be distinguished by their cross belts, worn from the left shoulder.

On 5 November 1605 the Yeomen of the Guard foiled the plot to blow up the Houses of Parliament when they discovered Guy Fawkes and his gunpowder in the cellars. Since 1679 the historic moment has been marked by a ritual in which the Yeomen search the chamber of the House of Lords and the Palace of Westminster cellars by lantern light before the State Opening of Parliament.

QUEEN'S APOTHECARY

It may come as a surprise in this scientific age that the medical division of the Royal Household includes Apothecaries among its members. The Queen's Apothecary is supported by the Apothecary to the Household and Apothecaries to the Households at Windsor and Sandringham. ¶ While today's royal apothecaries are fully qualified doctors, their predecessors practised skills acquired from millennia of knowledge of the medicinal benefits of plants. The earliest written records of the trade are Babylonian clay tablets from the third millennium BC that list instructions for mixing herbal prescriptions with which to treat illnesses. ¶ British monarchs sought the specialist skills of their apothecaries for centuries before science-based drugs so dramatically improved public health. But they looked to the Royal Apothecary to provide more than tinctures to cure agues. John Rumler, Apothecary to Charles I, 'compounded and served all sweet waters, perfumes and other odiferous things' for Queen Henrietta Maria. William Rosewell was Apothecary to Queen Catherine, wife of Charles II, and records exist of him seeking payment for preparing perfumes for her private chapel. Of course, no amount of herbal knowledge could delay death indefinitely, and one of the Royal Apothecary's most sombre duties was to supervise the embalming of the monarch's body. When Queen Mary died of smallpox in 1694, her apothecary Christian Harel used 'rich gummes and spices to stuff the body' and 'powders perfumed to lay in the coffin', according to his bill. ¶ The herbs and spices that were apothecaries' stock in trade led them to be part of the medieval Guild of Pepperers in the City of London, which maintained standards for the purity of spices and the setting of certain weights and measures. In 1428, the Pepperers were incorporated as the Worshipful Company of Grocers, reflecting the Pepperers' role as wholesale merchants dealing en gros – in bulk – from which comes 'grocer'. The London apothecaries petitioned for several years to secede from the Grocers' Company, led by the Apothecary to Anne of Denmark, wife of James I. This connection may well have influenced the King's granting of a Royal Charter to create the Worshipful Society of Apothecaries in 1617, whose motto is 'I am spoken of all over the world as one who brings help'. ¶ A landmark case in 1704 between the Society of Apothecaries and the Royal College of Physicians established the legal recognition of apothecaries as doctors able to prepare and dispense medicines.

The Queen's Apothecary in the surgery at Buckingham Palace Mews.

BNF
BNF
80
brother
How to Handwash?
DANGER
TiM

SURVEYOR OF THE QUEEN'S PICTURES

King Charles I was the most prolific and important collector of art of any British monarch. His collection of over 1,500 paintings and 500 sculptures encompassed some of the finest works of the Renaissance as well as commissions from contemporary artists such as Anthony van Dyck. To care for these treasures, Charles created the post of Surveyor of the King's Pictures in 1625. The first holder was Abraham van der Doort, whose duties included receiving and delivering the artworks, recording them in a register, protecting them from damage and arranging for copies to be made. The title 'Surveyor' was presumably chosen by analogy with a buildings surveyor, as the word 'curator' in the sense of an art custodian had not been coined at this date. ¶ Van der Doort committed suicide in 1640, devastated by his loss of one of the King's miniatures. Courtiers made unfortunate jokes about him hanging himself having previously hung others – in portrait form. Before his death, however, he created a catalogue of the King's collection, a copy of which survives in the Bodleian Library. This proved a vital document for the curators of the Royal Academy's 2018 landmark exhibition *Charles I: King and Collector*, which brought together over 100 works from the collection, which was sold off during the Interregnum. ¶ Many subsequent post-holders have also held other distinguished positions – often simultaneously. Benjamin West (in post 1791–1820) was also President of the Royal Academy; Richard Redgrave (in post 1856–80) was the first Keeper of Paintings at what became the Victoria and Albert Museum; William Seguier (in post 1820–43) and Kenneth Clark (in post 1934–44) were both also Directors of the National Gallery. Most notoriously, the Soviet spy Anthony Blunt (in post 1945–73) was simultaneously Director of the Courtauld Institute. ¶ Today, the Surveyor carries out much the same duties as those set out by Charles I. Chief among these is supervising conservation work, cataloguing the Royal Collection, devising and maintaining displays in the royal residences, approving loans and arranging temporary exhibitions at The Queen's Galleries. ¶ The million-plus objects in the Royal Collection are not owned privately by The Queen but are held in trust by the Sovereign for her successors and the nation. Many are on display at the principal royal residences, all of which are open to the public, while regular exhibitions give public access to further areas of the Collection. The oldest item in the Collection is the Rillaton Cup, an extremely rare early Bronze Age gold cup, which can be seen in the British Museum.

Previous page: The Surveyor of The Queen's Pictures sits in the 154-foot-long Picture Gallery in Buckingham Palace, where some of the greatest paintings in the Royal Collection are hung. The Picture Gallery was originally designed by John Nash for the magnificent art collection assembled by George IV and his predecessors, but also functions as one of the principal rooms for official entertaining and can accommodate several hundred guests at a time.

SURVEYOR OF THE QUEEN'S WORKS OF ART

The post of Surveyor of the Sovereign's Works of Art is a far more recent creation than that of the Surveyor of the Sovereign's Pictures: it was established within the Lord Chamberlain's Office by George V and Queen Mary in 1928. Queen Mary was a noted collector; through rigorous research she tracked down objects with historical links to the Royal Family in order to purchase them for the Royal Collection. ¶ The first post-holder was Sir Cecil Harcourt-Smith, an archaeologist who had previously been Director of the British School in Athens, Keeper of Greek and Roman Antiquities at the British Museum and Director of the Victoria and Albert Museum. He was succeeded in 1936 by Lieutenant-Colonel Lord Gerald Wellesley, a practising architect, but when his nephew was killed in action in 1943, he gave up the post to become the 7th Duke of Wellington. The role remained part-time, and was held by successive Directors of the Wallace Collection, until Sir Geoffrey de Bellaigue became the first full-time Surveyor in 1972. ¶ The Surveyor is the chief curator of decorative arts in the Royal Collection. With the decorative arts team of curators and conservators, the Surveyor is responsible for the presentation of furnishings and other decorative objects in the State Apartments, as well as planning conservation, contributing to exhibitions at The Queen's Galleries and carrying out research on the Collection. The Royal Collection receives no state funding or public subsidy. It is administered by the Royal Collection Trust, a registered charity, and income generated by the Trust from the public opening of Windsor Castle, Buckingham Palace, the Palace of Holyroodhouse and The Queen's Galleries supports its curatorial, conservation and educational work, loans, travelling exhibitions and public access projects. ¶ Together with the Director of the Royal Collection and the Crown Jeweller, the Surveyor also oversees the care of the Crown Jewels in the Tower of London.

Overleaf: The Surveyor of The Queen's Works of Art stands in The Queen's Gallery at Buckingham Palace. It was built on the site of a John Nash conservatory that was converted into a chapel for Queen Victoria in 1843. The chapel was destroyed in the Blitz, but in 1962 the site was redeveloped as a gallery for the Royal Collection at the suggestion of The Queen and The Duke of Edinburgh.

In December 2020 the Palace announced that 'The posts of Surveyor of The Queen's Pictures and Surveyor of The Queen's Works of Art will, for the time being, be lost and held in abeyance'. The Royal Collection Trust faced heavy financial losses as a result of the Covid-19 pandemic and the posts were cut as part of a voluntary severance programme.

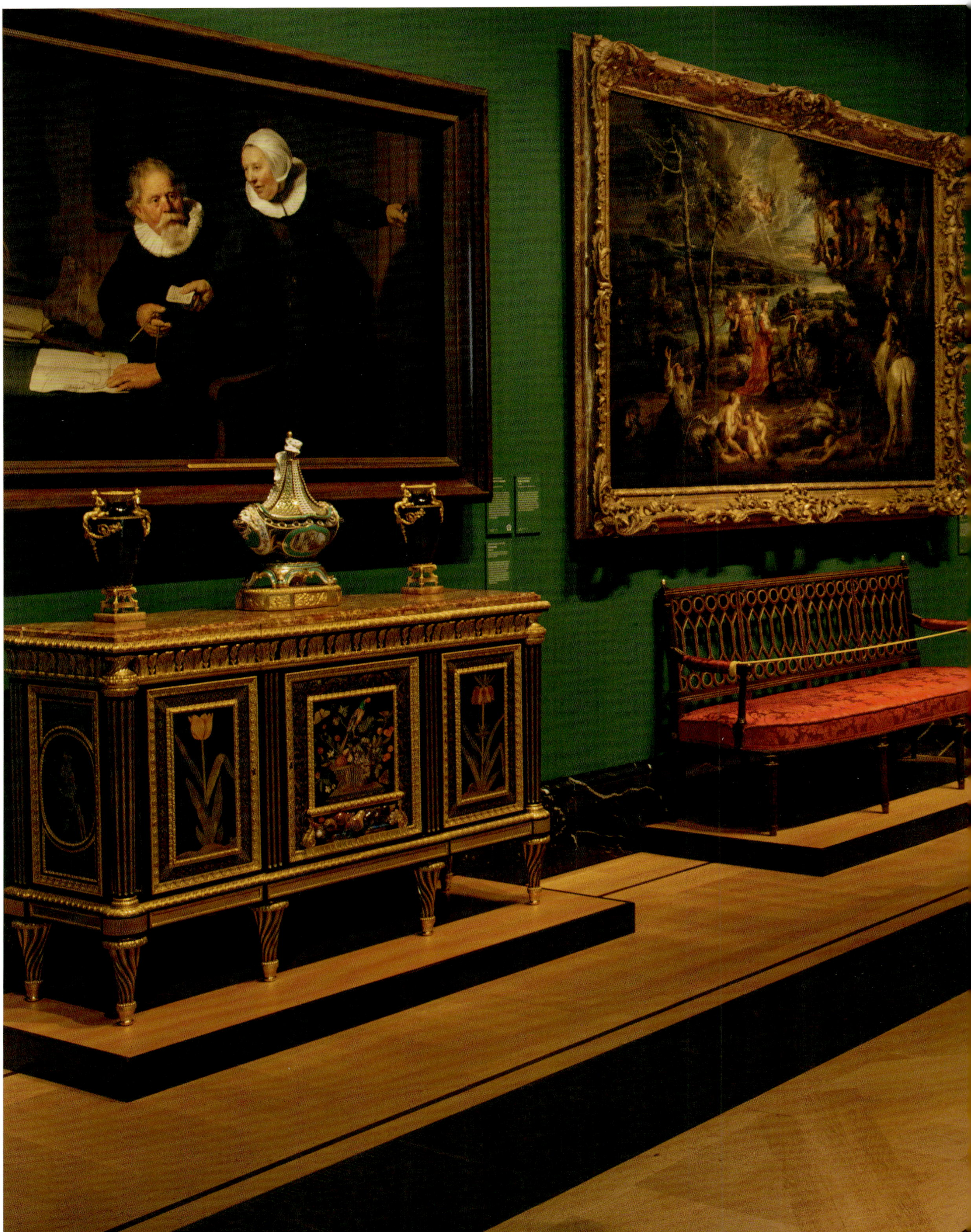

QUEEN'S GURKHA ORDERLY OFFICERS

The history of The Queen's Gurkha Orderly Officer dates back to 1876 when Queen Victoria was proclaimed Empress of India and the tradition of attendance on the Sovereign by six Indian Orderly Officers began. When Edward VII was crowned in 1902, he commanded that the Orderly Officers should consist not only of officers from Indian regiments but also from the Gurkha Brigade. Following the coronation the number was reduced to four and so, thereafter, four King's Orderly Officers were in attendance annually until the outbreak of the Second World War. In 1910, when King Edward died, these Indian Orderly Officers (two of whom were Gurkhas at the time) took turns to mount guard at one corner of the catafalque in Westminster Hall during the lying-in-state. The discipline, endurance and loyalty of the King's Indian Orderly Officers' vigil was recorded by Rudyard Kipling in his short story 'In the Presence'. ¶ On 11 March 1954, Queen Elizabeth reintroduced this practice by commanding that two Gurkha Officers be nominated annually from the Brigade of Gurkhas as Queen's Gurkha Orderly Officers and requiring them to attend her or other members of the Royal Family at official functions from time to time. ¶ Their primary responsibility is to attend investitures at royal residences as required. It is customary for The Queen to receive incoming Queen's Gurkha Orderly Officers in the Music Room on the first investiture day of the autumn season, when they present swords to The Queen. On investiture days The Queen's Gurkha Orderly Officers act as an escort from the door of the State Dining Room to the State Ballroom and position themselves on the Royal Dais. Throughout the ceremony they stand at attention, swords withdrawn. On the final investiture day, The Queen appoints Queen's Gurkha Orderly Officers to be Members of the Royal Victorian Order Fifth Class. ¶ Probably the best known, and to their adversaries the most feared, body of fighting men in the British Army, Gurkhas were first recruited to serve the Crown in 1815; for all those years their signature weapon has remained the Kukri. Since that time, these men from the Nepalese hills have fought in all the major wars where the British Army has been deployed, winning an extraordinary number of medals for bravery, including 13 Victoria Crosses since Nepalese members of the Brigade of Gurkhas became eligible in 1911. ¶ As Field Marshall Sam Manekshaw, former Chief of Staff of the Indian Army, once said, if a man says he is not afraid of dying, he is either lying or is a Gurkha.

The Queen's Gurkha Orderly Officers stand before the Chairs of Estate in the Throne Room of Buckingham Palace. The Queen's chair was made in 1953 for the Coronation and was used prior to the act of coronation itself.

QUEEN'S FLAG SERGEANT

When on duty, The Queen's Flag Sergeant enjoys some of the best views in the country, for it is his job to raise and lower the Royal Standard on the flagpoles of the principal royal residences to indicate The Queen's presence. ❡ The post is filled by a serving non-commissioned officer from the Household Division Brigade of Guards, which comprises the Life Guards, the Blues and Royals, Grenadier Guards, Coldstream Guards, Scots Guards, Irish Guards and Welsh Guards. The Flag Sergeant usually performs his duties for two years but this can be extended to four, and serves also as Steward to the Master of the Household. ❡ The raising of the Royal Standard coincides exactly with The Queen passing through the gates of Buckingham Palace, Windsor Castle, the Palace of Holyroodhouse or Balmoral Castle. The Flag Sergeant is in constant radio contact with the palace police control room and royal staff to time it down to the second. The Union Flag is flown when The Queen is not in residence, the size selected according to wind speed. ❡ The Royal Standard as we know it today dates to the reign of Queen Victoria, apart from minor changes. Earlier Royal Standards incorporated the Arms of Hanover but the Hanoverian association ended in 1837 with the accession of Victoria who, as a female, could not accede to Hanover. ❡ The Royal Standard is split into four quadrants: those at the top left and bottom right represent England with three gold lions on a red field; the top right quadrant represents Scotland and features a red lion rampant on a gold field; the bottom left quadrant represents Ireland with a gold harp on a blue field. Wales does not feature on the Royal Standard, as it is a Principality not a kingdom and thus pre-dates the Union of Ireland, Scotland and England by several hundred years. In Scotland the Royal Standard features two Scottish quadrants instead of the two representing England. ❡ The Flag Sergeant keeps an inventory of all the flags in his care, currently some 150 of different ages and sizes. The largest is the Anniversary Standard, which measures 38 by 19 feet and is flown on The Queen's Official Birthday, followed by the Garter Ceremony Standard, which is nearly half the size of a tennis court at 38 by 18 feet. The smallest are the car pennants. Others include the 24 by 12 foot State Visit flag, flown when Heads of State visit the palaces, and the Garden Party flag, a larger version of the 'everyday'

Previous page: The Queen's Flag Sergeant stands in the Ballroom at Buckingham Palace with an array of flags under his care. Directly below him is The Queen's personal flag, which she adopted in 1960. Whereas the Royal Standard represents not only the Sovereign but also the United Kingdom, The Queen's personal flag can only be flown by Her Majesty. It consists of the initial 'E' ensigned with the royal crown, surrounded by a chaplet of roses. The flag has effectively become The Queen's personal Commonwealth flag. It is flown to indicate her presence in non-monarchical Commonwealth countries and in realms that have not adopted a personal flag specifically for The Queen.

Royal Standard. ¶ The Flag Sergeant lives in the Royal Mews but travels with The Queen when she moves between the main royal residences. When Her Majesty has engagements abroad, he arranges for flags to be sent ahead to her destinations. ¶ Popular belief is that all flags should be flown at half mast upon the death of the monarch, but this convention does not apply to the Royal Standard. This illustrates the fact that at the very moment of the death of the Sovereign, the heir apparent immediately accedes to the throne, thereby ensuring uninterrupted succession. The Royal Standard is draped over the coffin of the Sovereign.

Previous page (top): The Queen reviews The King's Troop, Royal Horse Artillery in Hyde Park. This royal Range Rover bears the smallest version of the Royal Standard in the form of a pennant.

Previous page (bottom): The largest of the Royal Standards, the Anniversary Standard, flies over Buckingham Palace during The Queen's Birthday Parade.

Right: A small version of the Royal Standard is displayed on aircraft in which The Queen is travelling, but only when the plane is on the ground. In 1986 The Queen flew to China for her only State visit to that country. She wore yellow upon arrival, a colour that was traditionally reserved for Chinese emperors.

Bude Bay
Royal
Mail
CAAC

QUEEN'S PAGES OF HONOUR

When The Queen attends the State Opening of Parliament, she is accompanied by her four Pages of Honour who carry the lengthy train of her 18-foot crimson velvet Robe of State. The Pages are a visual reminder of the age of chivalry, when young sons of noble families would be sent to the castle or great house of another noble family to learn the principles of courtly and knightly behaviour. ¶ Medieval pages would serve their masters between the ages of seven and 14, performing duties such as delivering messages, serving at meals, cleaning clothes and weapons, while also receiving training in riding, hunting, falconry and combat – the essential skills for adult men of their rank. If required, some pages would accompany their lords into battle, providing support such as helping them put on their armour, or even rallying to the defence of a besieged castle. ¶ Of equally high regard was the acquisition of courtly manners, and the 'soft skills' of playing musical instruments, composing and singing songs, and learning board games such as chess. Pages could become squires from the age of 14, and potentially knights seven years later, but their time spent amid the family of a fellow nobleman would have endowed them with valuable social and political contacts that would endure for the rest of their lives. ¶ Today, a Page of Honour is a ceremonial position in the Royal Household that only requires attendance on State occasions, such as Coronations and ceremonies linked to the Orders of Chivalry. True to its medieval origins, however, it remains a distinction granted to pre-teen and teenage sons of members of the nobility and gentry, and also those of senior members of the Royal Household.

The Queen's Pages of Honour, pictured in the White Drawing Room in Buckingham Palace, wear a crimson coat decorated with gold buttons and brocade, a white satin waistcoat, white breeches and hose, white gloves, black buckled shoes and a lace cravat and ruffles. A short sword is also worn and the Pages are given a feathered three-cornered hat. The father of the Third Page of Honour (far right) was himself a Page of Honour from 1981 to 1983. The White Drawing Room is one of the more intimate State Rooms in the Palace, and is used for audiences and small gatherings. A hidden door formed from one of the four side cabinets and mirrors swings forward, giving The Queen access from the Royal Closet next door. The room will be familiar to millions who have watched The Queen's Christmas speech, which is often broadcast from here.

QUEEN'S PAGE OF HONOUR IN SCOTLAND

When The Queen attends the biennial service for the Most Ancient and Most Noble Order of the Thistle in Scotland, she is attended by The Queen's Page of Honour in Scotland. His primary role is to hold up the long train of The Queen's green velvet mantle during the grand procession to the Chapel of the Order of the Thistle in St Giles' Cathedral, Edinburgh, for the Order of the Thistle Service. The Page wears the same uniform as the Pages of Honour in England, comprising a white satin waistcoat, white breeches and hose, white gloves, black buckled shoes, a lace cravat and ruffles, and a court sword, although his gold-trimmed frock coat is made of green poplin.

The Queen's Page of Honour in Scotland stands in the ruined nave of Holyrood Abbey within the Palace of Holyroodhouse. The Abbey was founded in 1128 by Scotland's King David I. The cloister precinct was later turned into a 'modern' Renaissance palace – Holyroodhouse – and became the Royal Family's principal residence in Scotland. In Henry VIII's Reformation the choir and transepts were lost, but the nave became a Protestant parish church, surviving until the Catholic James VII and II evicted the worshippers in 1687.

QUEEN'S ARCHERS

In 1676 a private archery club was established in Edinburgh, and was granted the title the King's Company of Archers the following year by the Scottish Privy Council. In 1704 the company petitioned Queen Anne for a royal charter, becoming the Royal Company of Archers, by which they could assemble under the ancient dispensation of *wapinschaw* ('weapon-showing') with impunity. As payment for this privilege and for its endowment with 'perpetual access to all public butts, plains and pasturages legally allotted for shooting arrows', including the grounds at the Palace at Holyroodhouse, the Archers are expected to provide the Sovereign with three barbed arrows, if requested. ¶ When George IV became the first Hanoverian monarch to visit Scotland, in 1822, the Royal Company seized the opportunity to make its claim for the vacant position of Scotland's King's Body Guard. Throughout the visit the Archers escorted the King in State, and in recognition of their service George made their Captain-General the first Gold Stick for Scotland, and the Company became the Royal Company of Archers, King's Body Guard for Scotland. The royal visit was stage-managed by Company member and popular novelist of the day Sir Walter Scott. Because Scott was a member of the Royal Company of Archers, it is often thought that he helped design the somewhat fanciful uniform worn for the occasion, combining medieval and Elizabethan elements, such as puff sleeves and a ruff. When on ceremonial duty today members wear a more sober field uniform of dark green tunic with black facings, dark green trousers with black and crimson stripe, and a Balmoral bonnet with the Royal Company's badge and a golden eagle feather. ¶ While it remains an archery club, housed since 1777 at Archers' Hall in central Edinburgh, the Royal Company of Archers still serves as the Sovereign's Body Guard in Scotland, performing duties at the request of The Queen at State and ceremonial occasions held in Scotland. Every year the Royal Company attends Her Majesty's garden party at the Palace of Holyroodhouse, when some 120 members form avenues down which The Queen and The Duke of Edinburgh would walk and meet guests presented to them by the Company's Captain-General and President of the Council. Another important duty is attendance outside St Giles' Cathedral, Edinburgh, at the service of installation of Knights of the Thistle, and members attend investitures at the Palace of Holyroodhouse and the presentation of new Colours for Scottish regiments. ¶ Traditionally only a Scot may join the Company, or at least have strong Scottish connections, and all members are elected. Each member is still encouraged to be proficient with longbow and arrow and regular competitions are held to test their skills. Indeed, every summer, the Royal Company of Archers compete for the silver Musselburgh Arrow, believed to be the oldest continually held sporting event in the world since its formation in 1603.

Previous page: In the grounds of the Palace of Holyroodhouse The Queen's Archers display items of significance to the Royal Company. The member on the far left wears the field uniform and The Queen's Prize badge for winning the archery competition of the same name. Two golden eagle feathers denote the rank of Brigadier, to his right. Senior officer the Captain-General holds the Gold Stick for Scotland and wears three golden eagle feathers and the court uniform. The Match Secretary holds the silver Musselburgh Arrow that he won in 2016, and wears the '100 Prize' badge as the first member to win over 100 Royal Company archery prizes. On the far right, the Secretary's cap is distinguished by a Himalayan griffon vulture's feather. A Captain-General in the 1800s chose the tallest feather he could find to be able to distinguish the Secretary in a crowd.

Getty Images

King George VI, Queen Elizabeth, Princess Elizabeth, aged 11, and Princess Margaret, aged seven, talk to officers of the Royal Company of Archers, during an inspection at the Palace of Holyroodhouse in July 1937. Queen Elizabeth is in conversation with Lord Elphinstone, Captain-General of the Royal Company, who was also her brother-in-law, husband of her eldest sister Lady Mary.

Overleaf: The Queen's Bloodstock Adviser (left) and Sir Michael Stoute, one of The Queen's Racehorse Trainers, stand in the yard of Sir Michael's stables at Freemason Lodge, Newmarket. The Queen's Racing Colours are worn by three-time Champion Jockey Ryan Moore, whose wins include two Epsom Derbies, the Epsom Oaks, the St Leger Stakes and the Prix de l'Arc de Triomphe.

1895

EIIR

QUEEN'S BLOODSTOCK ADVISER, QUEEN'S RACEHORSE TRAINER AND QUEEN'S RACING COLOURS

Her Majesty The Queen is one of the most successful owners in the history of horseracing, with over 500 victories across flat and jump races. The only British Classic to elude her so far is the Epsom Derby, although her horse Aureole, bred by her father King George VI, took second place in the 1953 Derby. The Queen was named British flat racing Champion Owner in 1954 and 1957, the accolade for the owner whose horses have won the most prize money during a season, becoming the first reigning British monarch ever to do so twice. ¶ The Queen's passion for horseracing is clear for all to see at the racecourse, whether or not her horses are winning, and her knowledge and understanding of bloodstock is profound, developed over decades. She is guided by the professional insights of her Bloodstock Adviser, John Warren, based at the Highclere Stud in Berkshire. Mr Warren is the first person without a title or a military rank to become The Queen's Bloodstock Adviser, having taken over the role from his father-in-law, Henry Herbert, 7th Earl of Carnarvon, who held the position from 1969 until his death in 2001. ¶ The brood mares foal at the Royal Stud at Sandringham and photographs of the new foals with details of their birth and weight are sent to The Queen, who follows their progress closely. It is known that Her Majesty does not gamble on races, but indeed the breeding of racehorses is a form of gambling: studying the bloodlines, monitoring the horses' development, finessing their training, all culminating in the thrill of the race and the uncertainty of its outcome. ¶ The Royal Studs at Sandringham and Wolferton in Norfolk, and Polhampton Lodge in Hampshire, currently contribute to a training programme for around 25 horses racing each season. Sir Michael Stoute is one of The Queen's Racehorse Trainers, based in Newmarket, the capital of thoroughbred horseracing. His training career began in 1972; in nearly five decades, he has been ten times British flat-racing Champion Trainer and brought to victory the winners of 25 Classics in England and Ireland. In 2013 he trained The Queen's horse Estimate to a historic Gold Cup victory at Royal Ascot. ¶ The Queen's Racing Colours, worn by her jockeys, have represented the Royal Family at the racecourse since Edward VII introduced them in the late 19th century while Prince of Wales. Persimmon raced in the Prince of Wales's colours to win the 1896 Epsom Derby and St Leger. The colours, or silks, consist of a purple and scarlet jacket with gold braiding, with a black cap, and are provided by Gibson Saddles of Newmarket. The firm's association with the Royal Family began in 1932, when it was granted the Royal Warrant for providing racing colours to The Queen Mother. ¶ Ryan Moore, who wears the silks in this portrait, is one of The Queen's most successful flat-racing jockeys. He emerged as Champion Jockey in 2006, 2008 and 2009, and in 2013 he was in the saddle for Estimate's celebrated royal win at Ascot.

Getty Images

When The Queen's four-year-old filly Estimate won the Gold Cup at Royal Ascot in 2013, it was the first time in the race's 207-year history that the winning horse had been owned by a reigning monarch. Not since 1897 had a member of the Royal Family owned the winning horse – in that year victory went to Persimmon, owned and bred by the Prince of Wales, later King Edward VII. In 2020, The Queen missed Royal Ascot for the first time in her reign, when the Covid-19 pandemic meant the meet was held behind closed doors. Her horse Tactical won the Windsor Castle Stakes, however, giving The Queen her first win at Royal Ascot since 2016, when Dartmouth won the Hardwicke Stakes.

E II R
ROYAL LOFTS

QUEEN'S LOFTS MANAGER

The Sandringham Estate in Norfolk is home to some 250 racing pigeons, perhaps a lesser known part of The Queen's sporting life. Having owned pigeons since she was a child, she is extremely knowledgeable about the birds and pigeon racing, and is Patron of the Royal Pigeon Racing Association and the National Flying Club. ¶ The Royal Family has maintained a flock of racing pigeons since the very first were given to the then Prince of Wales, later Edward VII, by King Leopold II of Belgium in 1886. In the war years George VI allowed some of the royal birds to become carrier pigeons in the Army Pigeon Service, delivering messages to and from Europe. Indeed, in 1945, Royal Blue, one of the King's pigeons, was awarded a PDSA Dickin Medal for Gallantry (popularly known as the 'Animal Victoria Cross') in recognition that it was the first pigeon to bring a message from a force-landed aircraft on the Continent. ¶ Royal pigeons, bred and cared for by The Queen's Lofts Manager, compete regularly during the racing season from April to September, during which there may be as many as six races a week. They have an excellent success rate in both regional and national competitions; over the years, the Sandringham birds have won every major race in the north and south of the UK. During winter the Lofts Manager carries out the breeding programme and studies the birds' racing 'form' in preparation for the season. ¶ The Queen has often donated pigeons to charitable auctions to raise funds for causes as diverse as research into pigeon fancier's lung and the erection of the Animals in War Memorial on Park Lane.

The Queen's Lofts Manager holds a five-year-old pigeon that has won 13 races. The Lofts Manager spends 30 to 40 hours a week with the birds and sends The Queen a monthly report on their progress. The birds are identified by number rather than name, and the ring on their leg bears the Royal Cypher. The Royal Lofts built by George V were replaced in 2015 by state-of-the-art structures that are well ventilated and south-east facing to provide maximum sunlight for the birds.

QUEEN'S COMPANY GRENADIER GUARDS

The Queen's Company Grenadier Guards are widely reputed to be 'the finest of the finest' in the Guards Division. Her Majesty is the Company Commander and inspects the Company personally every ten years. The Queen's Company's actual name is the Sovereign's Company, its common parlance changing with the sex of each succeeding monarch. Their relationship with The Queen is a very special one, for while the troops of the Household Division guard The Queen's palaces and living body, The Queen's Company oversee the transition from one monarch to the next and undertake the exceptional role of guarding the body of the monarch in death too. It is for this reason that while other military units are retitled the King's Guard at the moment of accession, the Sovereign's Company remain the 'Queen's Company' until the moment following the actual burial of The Queen. They have the privilege of watching over the Sovereign's dead body prior to any public lying-in-state, and their 12 very best soldiers provide the bearer party at the Sovereign's funeral. The Company's Camp Colour (regimental flag) will be ritually placed by the new Sovereign on the coffin of the old at the end of the service. The Queen's Company also have the honour of being on duty in Westminster Abbey at the Coronation – the most solemn and mystical moment of monarchy. ¶ The richly hand-embroidered silk Queen's Company Colour (in the centre of the main portrait) is the oldest still in use by the Armed Forces, having been presented to the Company by Her Majesty on 14 April 1953 at Windsor Castle. Colours, Standards and Guidons are routinely replaced and presented to Armed Forces units every 10 years or so, but the Sovereign's Company will only ever receive one Colour during the monarch's lifetime. And while historical regimental colours of other units may be seen laid up after use in Britain's cathedrals, churches and school chapels, The Queen's Company Colour will be ritually folded and buried with the Sovereign. ¶ The Grenadier Guards are the most senior regiment of Foot Guards, having been formed as a Royalist regiment in 1656 while King-in-waiting Charles II was in exile in Bruges after the English Civil War. The Coldstream Guards may predate them in length of service to the nation, but did not swear allegiance to the Crown until the Restoration of the monarchy in 1660, which is why the Grenadier Guards are also referred to as the most senior infantry regiment in the British Army.

Previous page: Traditionally members of The Queen's Company had to stand over six feet tall, and The Queen's Company Stick (far right) was used as the minimum measurement for aspiring soldiers to beat. Although there is now no height restriction, the Company are still composed of the tallest, smartest members of every new intake to the regiment. The Queen's Company have a fearsome operational reputation and will be at the forefront of modern warfare engagements patrolling, delivering humanitarian relief and demonstrating first class infantry skills.

Since their foundation in 1660, The Queen's Company, the senior company of the Grenadier Guards, have carried a special Company Colour that is also the Royal Standard of the regiment. Larger than The Queen's and Regimental Colours, it is only carried when Her Majesty is present, and only ever lowered to her. The St Edward's Crown features centrally and above the badges of the rose of England, the Scottish thistle and the Irish shamrock in each corner.

QUEEN'S LONG GUARD

Every day of the year, whatever the season or weather, The Queen's Life Guard, made up of members of the Household Cavalry Mounted Regiment, ride from Hyde Park Barracks in Knightsbridge to take over guard duties at Horse Guards at 11 a.m. (Sundays at 10 a.m.). They will mount guard at Horse Guards in Whitehall, the official entrance to Buckingham and St James's Palaces, for 24 hours before handing over to the New Guard. The elegant white stone offices and stables designed by architect William Kent in 1750 are named after the troops who have mounted The Queen's Life Guard on that site in an unbroken tradition since the Restoration of King Charles II in 1660. ¶ The Household Cavalry Mounted Regiment consists of a squadron from each of the two most senior regiments of the British Army: The Life Guards wear red tunics and white plumed helmets, and The Blues and Royals wear blue tunics and red plumed helmets. As well as ceremonial duties these frontline soldiers are all fully trained in their operational armoured role as first line defence and reconnaissance on the battlefield, ready to be deployed whenever required at home and abroad. ¶ When Her Majesty is in London, indicated by the flying of the Royal Standard over Buckingham Palace, The Queen's Life Guard performs a Long Guard at Horse Guards Parade. This represents a reinforcement of security for the royal palaces and a greater degree of ceremonial pomp. A Long Guard consists of one trumpeter on a grey horse, one officer, one Corporal Major who carries the Standard, two non-commissioned officers and ten Troopers from the Household Cavalry Mounted Regiment, all mounted on cavalry black chargers. The trumpeter formally announces the arrival of The Queen's Life Guard by sounding a Royal Salute and leads them to their duties on Horse Guards Parade. ¶ The Standards carried so proudly by the soldiers on ceremonial duty historically acted as a rallying point during battle and now bear all the Battle Honours of both the Life Guards and the Blues and Royals. They embody within their magnificent silk and gold embroidery 400 years' history of service to the monarch and to the nation. ¶ A Short Guard is mounted by the Queen's Life Guard when The Queen is not in residence at Buckingham Palace, and is made up of two non-commissioned officers and ten Troopers.

Previous page: The trumpeter leads The Queen's Long Guard past Buckingham Palace and down The Mall to Horse Guards. Historically, the trumpeter rode a grey to increase his visibility on the battlefield in his role as the conveyor of orders and messages, a tradition that survives. The cavalry blacks are Irish Draught crossed with an element of thoroughbred and must be at least 16.2 hands high (5 feet 6 inches, measured from the ground to the highest point of the withers), while greys need only be 16 hands (5 feet 4 inches). The horses are reshod every two to six weeks, although some shoes are replaced after just seven days during the ceremonial season.

Soldiers were first employed as trumpeters in the Household Cavalry from the early 1660s with distinctive dress not unlike the State dress worn today. Ceremonial trumpeters are professional musicians and perform fanfares at important State occasions.

QUEEN'S GUARD

There are few more iconic images of London than the Changing of the Guard. Guard Mounting, as it is properly known, is where the Old Guard that has been guarding the Sovereign and the royal palaces exchanges duties with the New Guard. The immaculately smart service personnel who undertake this role are usually drawn from one of the regiments of the Foot Guards, but when they have operational commitments, it can fall to other units, other armed services or troops from the Commonwealth. ¶ Household Troops have guarded the Sovereign and the royal palaces in an unbroken tradition since 1660. The Changing of the Guard ceremony originally took place at the Palace of Whitehall, the Sovereign's official London residence until 1689. When the court moved to St James's Palace the ceremony moved with it. But when Queen Victoria took up residence in Buckingham Palace in 1837, The Queen's Guard remained at St James's Palace, with a detachment guarding Buckingham Palace as it does today. ¶ When The Queen is in residence at Buckingham Palace the number of sentries is increased. At 10.30 a.m. a detachment of the Old Guard mounts up at Friary Court and is inspected by the Captain of The Queen's Guard. They then leave St James's Palace and march down The Mall accompanied by a Band or Corps of Drums to Buckingham Palace. Meanwhile, the Old Guard at Buckingham Palace will be under inspection on the forecourt. At 10.43 a.m. the St James's Palace detachment joins them to await the arrival of the New Guard from Wellington Barracks. At 10.40 a.m. the Band at Wellington Barracks performs while awaiting the arrival of the Regimental Colour on parade, and for the New Guard to form up. They then all march out towards Buckingham Palace, arriving at 11 a.m. The Band plays the New Guard's Regimental slow march as it advances towards the Old Guard. After a 'present arms' the Captain of the Old Guard hands over the key to the Palace to the Captain of the New Guard, transferring all responsibilities. The officers continue their handover procedures in the Palace guardroom while the Ensigns bearing their Regimental Colours patrol the forecourt from left to right. Sentries are posted and given their duties while the Band plays. The relieved sentries complete the Old Guard, which, at 11.35 a.m., advances in slow time on the New Guard before exchanging compliments and departing for Wellington Barracks preceded by the Band, breaking into quick time as they leave the Palace. The New Guard divides into two. The detachment that is to guard St James's Palace departs with the remaining Corps of Drums to march down the Mall to lodge the Regimental Colour in the St James's Palace guardroom and assume their duties. The Buckingham Palace detachment retires to the guardroom to assume their duties there.

Previous page: The Old Guard of The Queen's Guard, leaving St James's Palace to be relieved of their duties. The Ensign carries the Regimental Colour of the Coldstream Guards.

QUEEN'S COLOUR

The lone flag that is at the heart of the annual Queen's Birthday Parade, borne by the regimental Ensign, is known as The Queen's Colour. In that rectangle of fabric is carried a regiment's history of military valour and loyalty to its monarch. So when one of the five Regiments of Foot Guards takes its turn to parade its Colour through the ranks, known as 'Trooping the Colour', it does so with pride at the continuation of a tradition of rallying to the Colour that can be traced back to the Middle Ages. ¶ The origins of The Queen's Colour lie in the Standards that were first recorded in the Battle of the Standard in 1138 when an English force repelled King David I of Scotland. The centre of the English line was marked by a ship's mast raised on a cart from which flew the consecrated banners of the great northern churches. The banners were a clearly visible point for the English soldiers to rejoin if separated from their comrades in the heat of battle. ¶ Under Queen Elizabeth I, when any 'low born captains in the infantry' lacked a coat of arms they adopted a plain coloured flag to distinguish them and their companies. These flags became known as Colours. In 1747 it was ordained that each battalion should have only two Colours: the King's Colour (the Union Flag) and the Regimental Colour. The Foot Guards, however, retained an earlier tradition of the King's Colour bearing the regimental crest or badge, while the Regimental Colour was the Union Flag. ¶ The Battle Honours emblazoned on The Queen's Colour are a visual embodiment of the military endeavours of a regiment, its spirit and sacrifice. The Colour is revered for all that it symbolises, and when it is replaced it is usually laid up in a church significant to that regiment.

The Ensign of Nijmegen Company of the Grenadier Guards lowers The Queen's Colour in salute to their Sovereign at The Queen's Birthday Parade.

1916 2016

QUEEN'S FLIGHT

The Royal Family has had an interest in aviation since its earliest days. King Edward VII met flight pioneers Wilbur and Orville Wright in Paris in 1909 and watched them demonstrate their 'Flyer' biplane. The Prince of Wales (later Edward VIII) made his first flight in 1916, but when his father King George V heard that the Prince had been flown by a pilot with one arm in a sling in 1918, he banned his heir from flying. Edward's brother Albert (later George VI) joined the RAF in 1919 and became the first member of the Royal Family to be certified as a fully qualified pilot. In the 1920s Edward was finally allowed to take flying lessons and became a keen aviator. ¶ The first two aircraft ordered specifically for transportation of the Royal Family, unofficially known as the Royal Flight, were delivered to No. 24 Squadron at RAF Northolt in April 1928. When Edward was proclaimed King on 20 January 1936, he flew from Sandringham to London, thus becoming the first British monarch to travel by air. The Royal Flight officially became The King's Flight in July 1936, by which time No. 24 Squadron was based at RAF Hendon. As the world's first head of state aircraft unit, it initially used the King's privately owned aircraft, but after the King abdicated in December 1936 an Airspeed Envoy was bought with public funds. The outbreak of war led to the disbanding of The King's Flight in 1942, but it was reformed in 1946 at RAF Benson. ¶ Becoming The Queen's Flight in 1952 upon the accession of Queen Elizabeth II, the unit operated a variety of aircraft for the transportation and pilot training of members of the Royal Family, and in 1953 Prince Philip made the first royal flight in a helicopter. In 1986 three VIP-configured BAe 146-100s entered service with The Queen's Flight as its first jet aircraft. ¶ On 1 April 1995, The Queen's Flight was merged into No. 32 Squadron to become No. 32 (The Royal) Squadron, based at RAF Northolt. This brought an end to the RAF's provision of dedicated VIP transport aircraft, as the squadron's aircraft are only available to VIP passengers if not needed for military operations. In 2004 the squadron's jets lost their distinctive red livery inherited from The Queen's Flight, over concern for the aircraft's vulnerability to terrorist attack. ¶ The Queen does not travel on scheduled flights, but the rest of the family does whenever possible, although royal protocol dictates that two heirs to the British throne should not travel together.

Previous page: Members of No. 32 (The Royal) Squadron – The Queen's Flight – at RAF Northolt, with a BAe 146 aircraft bearing the squadron's insignia. The badge of a stringed hunting horn, signifying the unit's ability to hunt the enemy, was approved by King George VI in December 1936. Opened in 1915 as the Royal Flying Corps' Military School, Northolt is the RAF's oldest station. In 1940 it played a vital part in the airborne Battle of Britain and was home to Polish fighter squadrons.

QUEEN'S COLOUR SQUADRON

The Queen's Colour Squadron, the elite ceremonial unit of the Royal Air Force Regiment, is tasked with the care and protection of The Queen's Colour for the RAF (pictured below in badge form). It was created on 1 November 1960, when the Royal Air Force Drill Unit, in existence since the early 1920s, was renamed. The first Colour presented to the RAF was bestowed on 26 May 1951 by Princess Elizabeth on behalf of her father, King George VI. ¶ For the first 30 years of its existence, The Queen's Colour Squadron fulfilled a purely ceremonial role, providing the sole escort to the Colour, and was renowned for its exhibition drill displays, performed without a single word of command. In the Armed Service reforms of 1990 it took on an operational role as a field squadron and was renamed The Queen's Colour Squadron RAF (No. 63 Squadron RAF Regiment). ¶ The Squadron is still famed for its drill displays, and took a prominent part in the centenary celebrations of the RAF in 2018. It provided the Escort Squadron on the forecourt of Buckingham Palace for the Centenary Parade on 10 July 2018, when all seven Queen's Colours were paraded. The RAF's new Colour, marking its 100th year, was presented to the Squadron by The Queen, after which the Squadron performed a special drill to form the wording 'RAF 100'. ¶ The Queen's Colour Squadron's ceremonial duties include mounting The Queen's Guard on behalf of the RAF at the London palaces and Windsor Castle, and providing Guards of Honour for the Royal Family, heads of state, dignitaries and other VIPs.

QUEEN'S BARGEMASTER AND ROYAL WATERMEN

The earliest record of an English monarch travelling by royal barge dates to 1215 when King John was conveyed along the Thames to Runnymede by a bargemaster and his watermen to put his seal to Magna Carta. London's great river was a vital transport route during centuries when roads were poorly maintained and congested. Indeed, it was faster and safer for the Sovereign, members of the Royal Family and courtiers to move between the royal palaces of Westminster, the Tower of London, Greenwich, Windsor and Hampton Court by royal barge than by carriage. ¶ Tradition dictates that an act of piracy in the early 1300s led to the formal royal appointment of watermen. Edward II was rescued by his watermen when a band of pirates attacked him while he was taking exercise by rowing on the River Fleet, a tributary of the Thames. An Act of Parliament in 1514 regulated the fares charged by Thames watermen for ferrying passengers, but it was not until a further Act was passed in 1555 that licences and further regulations were imposed and the Company of Watermen of the River Thames created. In 1700 lightermen (carriers of goods) joined the Company. ¶ With the improvement of roads in the 19th century carriages replaced royal barges as the preferred means of moving the Sovereign through London. Today there are 24 Royal Watermen, led by The Queen's Bargemaster; they are chosen from the ranks of Thames watermen who still work on the river operating launches, lighters and tugs. The Royal Watermen serve as coachmen on duties that would formerly have involved the Royal Barge, such as State visits, royal weddings and jubilees. They are most visible at the State Opening of Parliament. On this occasion The Queen's Bargemaster and four Royal Watermen travel as footmen on the carriages bearing the regalia, which used to arrive by river – the Imperial State Crown, Sword of State, maces and Cap of Maintenance. It is the duty of the Bargemaster to pass the crown to the Comptroller upon arrival at the Palace of Westminster. ¶ Whenever The Queen or members of the Royal Family travel ceremonially along the Thames, they are accompanied by the Bargemaster and Royal Watermen. The Bargemaster chooses eight Watermen when The Queen is on board, as eight oarsmen used to propel the fastest of the old shallop barges.

The Queen's Bargemaster and a Royal Waterman stand at the Sovereign's Entrance, at the foot of the Victoria Tower in the Palace of Westminster, which is used by The Queen whenever entering the Palace. The steps leading to the Norman Porch mark the start of the processional route taken by The Queen for the State Opening of Parliament. The Queen's Bargemaster is distinguished by his white stockings, worn with an early form of court dress emblazoned front and back with a silver gilt Royal Cypher plastron. The Royal Waterman, who holds the Royal Standard flown at the Palace of Westminster for the State Opening, wears a 14th-century-style skirted scarlet tunic with a similarly emblazoned jacket and scarlet stockings.

QUEEN'S SWAN MARKER

One of The Queen's more arcane titles is 'Seigneur of the Swans', denoting a historic link between the monarch and this most noble of birds. There may be a popular misconception that The Queen owns all the swans in the land, but there is a grain of truth in this belief linked to the role of The Queen's Swan Marker. ¶ The reigning monarch can claim ownership of any unmarked mute swans on open water or can give such rights to others. No records exist of when this custom began, other than there is written evidence dating to around 1186 of a number of captive swans belonging to Henry II, probably kept both for their beauty and their culinary worth. Swans were a prized feast dish, particularly at Christmas; 40 swans were ordered for Henry III's Christmas celebrations in 1247 in Winchester. To preserve swans' exclusivity, in 1482 it was ordained that only landowners of a certain wealth could keep them. A system of identification was devised, whereby the upper beaks were nicked with unique marks, the earliest records of which date to about 1400. The significant cost of purchasing swan marks meant that ownership was restricted to the monarch, rich landowners and institutions such as cathedrals and trade guilds. Today, besides The Queen, only three bodies still own swans: the Ilchester Estate, whose Abbotsbury Swannery in Dorset was founded in the mid-1300s by Benedictine monks, and the Vintners' and Dyers' livery companies. ¶ A Swan Upping ceremony evolved under the office of Swan Marker, during which swan families were rounded up for marking and assessment. The ceremony is still held on the Thames over five days in July, led by The Queen's Swan Marker. Uniformed Swan Uppers travel 79 miles between Sunbury in Surrey and Abingdon in Oxfordshire in six traditional wooden skiffs, two each for the Crown, the Vintners and the Dyers. When a swan family is spied, Uppers cry 'All-Up!' and surround the birds with their flag-bedecked boats, until they are able to lift them out of the water. On shore, the Swan Marker establishes ownership of the adults and allocates the brood. These days the liveries mark their birds with rings, while The Queen's swans are unmarked. ¶ The Swan Marker's role uniquely combines ceremony with conservation. Given the threats faced by the birds, Swan Upping is a vital opportunity both to monitor their health and to educate the public on protecting the river environment. In 1985, only seven breeding pairs were recorded on the London to Henley stretch. Lead poisoning was partly to blame for their drastic decline, and a ban on lead fishing weights has helped their recovery. During Swan Upping, schoolchildren meet the Swan Marker and the Uppers to learn about swans and river ecology, so that they too will become champions of these regal birds.

The Queen's Swan Marker wears a swan quill in his cap and holds a mute swan on the banks of the River Thames at Cookham Lock in Berkshire.

QUEEN'S CHAPLAINS

The role of Royal Chaplain can be traced back to Saxon times, but the office has evolved considerably over the centuries. The Royal Chaplains are headed by the Clerk of the Closet, and the first recorded holder of that office dates to 1437, one Edward Atherton. The Clerk of the Closet acted as confessor to the Sovereign and would thus have been a most trusted individual. The Closet would have been a small secure place, an exclusive inner sanctum within the Chapels Royal set aside for the more private devotions of the Sovereign. The Closet in St James's Palace, for example, is located in the balcony of the Chapel Royal. From the 1500s the influence of Clerks of the Closet was so great that bishops were generally selected for the office, though this only became the norm from 1714, when the Bishop of Winchester was appointed to guide George I. ¶ The Royal Chaplains are chosen by the Sovereign from a list of names supplied by the Clerk of the Closet. They are selected from all over the country and automatically become members of the College of Chaplains to the Sovereign, founded in 1912 after reforms instigated by Edward VII, with an upper limit of 36 members. Historically, these priests were, in effect, representing the voice and authority of the Sovereign around the realm from their pulpits. Their role was particularly significant during the tumultuous years of the Reformation, while their promulgation of the King James Bible issued in 1611 and the 1662 Book of Common Prayer, following the Restoration of King Charles II, was critical to embedding these Protestant texts into people's daily practice of faith. When preaching according to the Royal Household Rota of Waits, or roll of duty preachers, The Queen's Chaplains still draw upon these ancient Formularies of the Church. ¶ The Clerk of the Closet is supported by the Deputy Clerk, who is also the Domestic Chaplain to the Sovereign and the only full-time clerical member of the Sovereign's Ecclesiastical Household; the other Chaplains serve in parishes or faith-based roles up and down the country. ¶ The Queen's Chaplains are invited to preach annually at the Chapel Royal, St James's Palace, or in The Queen's Chapel nearby, and once appointed, they remain in post until the age of 70. Today The Queen's Chaplains are a highly visible statement of an effective ministry recognised by the Sovereign as being of particular significance in the loyal service they give to their local communities or organisations in which they serve.

It is believed that at the Reformation Henry VIII decided to dress his Chaplains in scarlet as a visible gesture to the Pope and his cardinals. The Queen's Chaplains continue to enjoy the distinction of being permitted to wear scarlet cassocks along with white preaching bands attached to their clerical collars and a silver-gilt Badge of Office that incorporates a blue-enamelled Royal Cypher and bow surrounded by a laurel oak motif. The Chapel Royal at Hampton Court Palace boasts one of the most magnificent timber and plaster ceilings in Britain, all that remains of the Tudor decoration.

QUEEN'S ALMSMEN

During his reign Henry VII, the first Tudor monarch, built an almshouse close to the west end of Westminster Abbey near the Great Gatehouse, and endowed it with provision for 13 almsmen, 'poor men decayed in the King's service', including one priest, plus three serving women. The first almsmen began their service in 1502, receiving their annual allotment of robes in time for the feast of All Saints on 1 November. Under Queen Elizabeth I, the almsmen's duties were 'to pray for the Queen's majesty, for the Church, and for the peace and safety of the kingdom'. ¶ The almshouse was demolished long ago and The Queen's Almsmen, now numbering six, no longer live within the Abbey precinct. They are appointed by The Queen and are required to attend the Dean of Westminster Abbey during Sunday services and on special occasions such as memorial services and royal weddings. On Sundays they take the collection and carry it to the medieval Jericho Parlour and place it in a safe. They process behind the Dean, and behind members of the Royal Family if they are present. ¶ One of the criteria for selection of almsmen has been that they should have served in the Armed Forces. In the past it was possible to recruit from ex-military members of the Abbey staff, but now there are very few ex-service personnel on the staff and the net is cast wider. The first woman to be appointed as a Queen's Almsman is Mariama Ifode-Blease, who began her duties at the Abbey in January 2014. Rather than a military background, Dr Ifode-Blease holds a DPhil in Spanish from Cambridge University and works in the education sector. Her fellow almsmen include Michael Dyer JP, who has spent 20 years serving the Dioceses of London and Southwark and is Bursar of the Society of Saint John the Evangelist; Alex McBride, who was an officer in the London Scottish Territorial Army; and Chelsea Pensioner John Bassett.

The Queen's Almsmen are strikingly visible within Henry VII's Lady Chapel at Westminster Abbey in their scarlet gowns, emblazoned on the shoulder with the silver badge of a crowned Tudor rose on a blue background. They may also wear any medals they have been awarded. The chapel was described by the 16th-century historian John Leland as 'the wonder of the world'. Beneath its glorious medieval fan-vaulted ceiling are buried 15 kings and queens including Elizabeth I, Mary Queen of Scots, Charles II, Queen Anne and George II. Work began in 1503 with generous funds provided by Henry VII, but was not completed until 1516, nearly six years after his death. His own tomb bears magnificent gilt bronze effigies of the King and his wife, Elizabeth of York, both of whom lie in a vault below their monument. The colourful heraldic banners of the Knights of the Order of the Bath hang above the misericords, and since 1725, when George I revived the ancient order, the chapel has been designated the Chapel of the Order of the Bath and is used for installations of the Knights.

HNS PEMBRO
ADMIRALTY PILOT
SD CLYDE RACER

QUEEN'S HARBOUR MASTER

The primary purpose of The Queen's Harbour Master is to protect the port for which he is responsible, the Royal Navy and its vessels and other government assets. The post of The Queen's Harbour Master was formally established in law by the Dockyard Ports Regulation Act of 1865, in the reign of Queen Victoria, although the title had existed for some time before that. From 1814, the title appeared in Naval Records; although the office of Master Attendant was an older form, the two titles seemed interchangeable from the early 1800s. The first recorded King's Harbour Master was James Park at Portsmouth in 1816, and in 1860 an Admiralty Order in Council gave the rank of Commander to the post of The Queen's Harbour Master. ¶ While the British Naval Dockyards at the time all had appointed Queen's Harbour Masters (Chatham, Deptford, Pembroke, Plymouth, Portsmouth, Rosyth, Sheerness and Woolwich), some overseas Royal Navy ports also had Queen's Harbour Masters (such as Malta, Gibraltar, Port Edward in the British territory of Wei-hai-Wei in north-east China, and Halifax in Novia Scotia). Today the numbers are much reduced to Portsmouth and Plymouth in England, Clyde in Scotland, East Cove Port on East Falkland, and Gibraltar. ¶ A Queen's Harbour Master is appointed by the Secretary of State for Defence to superintend the Act and protect the Dockyard Port. The main role is to ensure that any activity in Dockyard Port waters is conducted safely and meets the requirements of the customers who may be either military, commercial or leisure. This might range from organising and conducting the docking of a nuclear submarine, to assessing and approving a plan for a charity swim, responding to an oil spill from a vessel, liaising with foreign navies for support arrangements for their warships or dealing with legal issues over the salvage of a sunken ship. No two days are ever the same, and much of the dialogue takes place with port users in the wider area. The Clyde Dockyard Port, for example, covers Gareloch, Loch Long and Loch Goil, with outlying Ministry of Defence-owned facilities as far afield as Loch Ewe in the north-west Highlands.

The Queen's Harbour Master aboard his pilot vessel in the busy waters of the Dockyard Port at Her Majesty's Naval Base Clyde, Faslane. Alongside the Red Ensign, his pilot vessel flies The Queen's Harbour Master's own flag, created in 1915: a white-bordered Union flag with a white circle on it, within which is the Tudor crown and the letters 'QHM'.

HBM
DIPLOMATIC
SERVICE

TRANSIT
CUSTOM
HBM
DIPLOMATIC
SERVICE
HBM
DIPLOMATIC
SERVICE
HBM
DIPLOMATIC
SERVICE

QUEEN'S MESSENGERS

Since ancient times governments have relied on the efficient and secure communication of commands and policies. The Corps of Queen's Messengers links this highly valued duty from centuries past to the present day. ¶ The first written mention of Royal Messengers appeared during the rule of King John in 1199, although the office will have existed for centuries beforehand. Those entrusted were noblemen or favoured courtiers, and they performed a range of services from collecting taxes to escorting those accused of High Treason, including Henry VIII's queens Anne Boleyn and Catherine Howard. They even carried the body parts of traitors around the kingdom for public display. Medieval heralds acted as Royal Messengers and were sometimes entrusted with basic tasks of diplomacy. In later centuries, Messengers served as the Sovereign's private police force conducting investigations as directed. During both world wars, King's Messengers carried secret communiqués to and from Germany, thus playing their part in the Allied victories. ¶ Royal Messengers were part of the Royal Household until 1824 when operational control was passed to the then Foreign Office. However, a Royal Messenger was required to be on standby wherever the Sovereign was resident well into the 1930s. ¶ The Corps of Queen's Messengers remains one of the most experienced and respected courier services in the world. It is responsible for the effective and secure international delivery of the United Kingdom's classified diplomatic material under the protection of the Vienna Convention of 1961. Today, some 17 Queen's Messengers travel the globe by air, land and occasionally sea in all temperatures and climates, collectively covering hundreds of thousands of miles each year. The Corps' motto is still highly appropriate: 'Neither snow nor rain nor heat nor gloom of night shall stay these couriers in the swift completion of their appointed rounds' (Herodotus).

Previous page: The diplomatic bags for which The Queen's Messengers are responsible never leave their sight. Under the terms of the Vienna Convention for Diplomatic Relations, bags containing official government communications can be carried by appointed people without fear of interference, so are exempt from customs inspection. The Queen's Messenger, helped by a driver, loads diplomatic bags at the Foreign, Commonwealth and Development Office on Whitehall; 'HBM' stands for 'Her Britannic Majesty'.

The Queen's Messengers are entitled to the Badge of Office, which is the Sovereign's Royal Cypher with a silver greyhound suspended below. It is thought that Henry VII chose this canine emblem when he ordered the greyhound of Richmond to be one of the heraldic beasts to support his royal arms, and, perhaps to inspire them to speed, it was embroidered on the tunics of the Tudor Messengers. Charles II, in looking to safeguard the security of his letters while in exile in the Netherlands, broke off silver greyhounds decorating a dish and gave them to his Messengers as proof of their credentials. The number of Queen's Messengers has increased in recent years as they need to hand-carry sensitive Foreign Office documents to avoid computer hacking and cyber espionage.

QUEEN'S REMEMBRANCER

The Queen's Remembrancer, together with the Chancellor of the Exchequer, are the only two extant appointments from the time of the Court of the Exchequer, which was established by Henry I in the early 1100s. The Court collected revenue from the King's subjects, and Henry II created the post of King's Remembrancer in 1154 to 'put the King in remembrance of all things owing to the King', in other words to keep a check on revenues delivered by the Sheriffs of the shires to the monarch. Richard of Ilchester, later to become Bishop of Winchester, was the first King's Remembrancer. ¶ In 1834 the office of The Queen's Remembrancer became the responsibility of the Senior Master of the Exchequer. When the Court of the Exchequer was abolished in 1873, the Senior Master of the Exchequer became the Senior Master of the new Supreme Court, and as Queen's Remembrancer, performed the remaining functions of the Court of the Exchequer. Today, the Remembrancer's most significant role is Senior Master of The Queen's Bench Division, one of three divisions of the High Court, covering commercial and maritime law, serious personal injury, breach of contract, defamation and professional negligence. ¶ When the Lord Chancellor ceased to have a judicial role in 2005, the office of The Queen's Remembrancer became the oldest judicial post in continual existence since the Middle Ages, yet it still bears many other pertinent responsibilities. These include hearing the declarations of office of the Sheriffs of the City of London and delivering their warrants from The Queen, and suing in the courts for fines imposed by the House of Lords, the Court of Appeal and the High Court. ¶ The Remembrancer holds custody of the Great Seal of the Exchequer. When there is a change of Chancellor of the Exchequer, a complicated manoeuvre must be accomplished swiftly so that Treasury business can resume. The seal must be returned by the Remembrancer to the outgoing Chancellor, who must then return it to The Queen, who in turn delivers it to the new Chancellor, who finally returns it to the Remembrancer. ¶ Every year the Remembrancer oversees the Trial of the Pyx, a ceremony dating to 1249. The Remembrancer swears in a jury of 26 goldsmiths at Goldsmiths' Hall, who must count, weigh and measure a sample of gold coins made by the Royal Mint, and deliver their verdict to the Remembrancer.

In 2014 the Honourable Ms Justice Barbara Fontaine became the first woman to hold the post of The Queen's Remembrancer. As such, she is the only judge in England and Wales to wear a baron's tricorn hat, symbolising that the Court of the Exchequer was once filled with barons. The Queen's Remembrancer, with the tools of the Trial of the Pyx, holds a £550 gold coin in Goldsmiths' Hall. She is accompanied by the Beadle (left) and Prime Warden of the Goldsmiths' Company.

HONI SOIT QUI MAL Y PENSE

QUEEN'S COUNSELS

A body of lawyers known as 'His (or Her) Majesty's learned counsel' emerged from the Offices of the Attorney General and Solicitor General by the end of the 17th century, appointed by the Crown to assist the law officers. The first Queen's Counsel (QC) to be established by patent was the polymath Francis Bacon, whose legal mind Queen Elizabeth I rated so highly she reserved him for her exclusive use. ¶ The Stuart kings appointed further King's Counsels, and as numbers increased they effectively ceased to be counsel to the Crown, becoming rather a class of counsel ranked superior to ordinary barristers by virtue of talent or favour. ¶ Today, the raising of a barrister (or solicitor) in England and Wales to the rank of QC recognises that they are 'considered as experts in their field', in the words of the Bar Standards Board. The appointment can be seen as a form of quality control, offering potential clients some guidance as to the level of experience and abilities of the advocates they intend to instruct. ¶ Junior barristers put themselves forward for the rigorous and highly competitive selection process, and appointments are ultimately made by a nine-person selection panel composed of legal and lay members. In 2003, this system replaced the previous process whereby QC appointments were made by The Queen on the Lord Chancellor's recommendation, who in turn may either have known candidates personally from his Bar career or been advised of their talents by other QCs. Only one in ten junior barristers goes on to become a Queen's Counsel, thereby advancing from the Outer Bar to the Inner Bar and a place in the front row of the court. ¶ Applicant numbers have dropped dramatically in recent years, but even now, fewer than half of those who apply are approved, representing the best of their generation. Motivation is provided by the knowledge that without the letters QC after their name they are unlikely to be picked to lead the legal team in the biggest cases. ¶ It took over 350 years since Bacon's elevation to QC for Helena Normanton to become the first woman to be admitted to an Inn of Court, after the passing of the Sex Disqualification (Removal) Act 1919. She was made a KC in 1949, as was Rose Heilbron, who also gave birth to her daughter Hilary in the same year; Hilary became a QC too. Over a century on from the Act, only 15 per cent of practising QCs are women.

Previous page: Queen's Counsels in the Great Hall of the Royal Courts of Justice on the Strand. The ceremony at which Queen's Counsels are formally appointed is known as taking Silk, since they replace their woollen gown with a silk gown, gaining the colloquial moniker Silks. They also wear a long, full-bottomed wig, stockings and breeches, the latter of which are optional for women. The ceremony requires of a new member of the Inner Bar an Oath, a handshake with the Lord Chancellor and the costly purchase of Letters Patent recording their new status and exact position in the order of precedence of practitioners.

The red cloth 'brief bag' belonging to Adrienne Page QC is used to carry her QC wig and robes and papers. In England, brief bags are either blue or red, and the distinction is telling. Junior barristers may provide themselves with a blue brief bag when they are first called to the Bar, while only Silks may purchase red ones. However, red brief bags can be given by QCs to junior barristers (or sometimes solicitors) with whom they have worked in recognition of their contribution to a case, usually one that has concluded favourably. As such, they are viewed as a badge of merit and it is considered an honour to receive one from a grateful QC.

17

QUEEN'S SCOUTS

Queen's Scouts have attained the highest youth award achievable in the Scouting movement in the Commonwealth: The Queen's Scout Award (QSA). Its origins date to October 1909 when the founder of the Boy Scouts, Lieutenant-General Robert Baden-Powell, during a visit to Balmoral, had a long conversation about the Scouts with King Edward VII. When Baden-Powell suggested that boys who passed special efficiency tests should be ranked as King's Scouts, the King assented. In order to be a King's Scout a boy had first to become a First Class Scout by passing ten tests, and then pass another four out of seven badges. By 1910 over 1,600 King's Scout Badges had been issued out of nearly 100,300 Scouts. ¶ In 1966 the Venture Scout Section was launched for 16–20-year-old Scouts, and they became eligible to gain The Queen's Scout Award by completing a wide range of achievements to gain the Venture Award and then developing some of these to a higher standard. In 1976 girls were admitted to Venture Scouts and also became eligible to gain the QSA. In 2003 the Venture Scout Section was replaced by the Explorer Scout programme for 14–18 year olds and the Scout Network for 18–25 year olds. ¶ Today, to gain the Award Explorer Scout or Scout Network members must take part in various demanding challenges that test qualities such as self-reliance, determination and self-discipline. ¶ Each year only about 500 young people across the UK gain the QSA. On a Sunday close to St George's Day, new Queen's Scouts gather with holders of Adult Awards and Meritorious Conduct and Gallantry Awards at Windsor Castle for an annual parade, a privilege granted by King George V in 1934. The salute is often taken by a member of the Royal Family, and after the parade the National Scouts Service is held at St George's Chapel on a theme chosen and prepared by Scouts. ¶ Every Queen's Scout receives a royal certificate bearing this message from Her Majesty: 'As a Queen's Scout you have prepared yourself for service to God and other people, and have shown yourself a worthy Member of the worldwide Scout Movement. I wish you God-speed on your journey through life; may it prove for you a joyous adventure.' Since 1952 well over 50,000 Queen's Scout Certificates have been presented to young men and women who have qualified for this coveted Award.

Previous page: Ferny Crofts is a 31-acre Scout Activity Centre in the heart of the New Forest National Park, owned by Hampshire County Scout Council, some 30 of whose members become Queen's Scouts every year. The first Hampshire Scout Camp took place here in 1976. The Queen's Scout second from right wears the blue diamond-shaped badge of The Queen's Scout Award.

QUEEN'S GUIDE TO THE SANDS

Until the railway arrived in the 1850s, crossing the treacherous Kent Sands of Morecambe Bay by foot or cart was the only way to avoid the long and badly maintained coast road. The bay's infamously fast tides have claimed many lives, with the unwary being caught out by the dykes and gullies, channels and quicksand over which the tidal water floods from east and west. The risk of drowning was so real the Abbot of Furness Abbey, on the west side of the bay, petitioned King Edward II in 1326 to investigate the great loss of life. The Crown recognised the need for an official guide to the bay at least as early as the 16th century: the first recorded office holder, then known as the Carter upon Kent Sands, was Edmonstone, who was appointed in 1501. ¶ The earliest Carters were paid by the Prior of Cartmel, an outpost of Furness Abbey, but in 1537, during Henry VIII's Dissolution of the Monasteries, Furness's land holdings and wealth were transferred to the Duchy of Lancaster, which became and remains the Guide's paymaster. ¶ The post came with a bay-facing 10-acre tenement at Cartmel, called Guide's Farm, where the longest-serving Queen's Guide lived until his retirement in 2019 at the age of 86. Cedric Robinson, a local fisherman by trade, applied for the job in 1963, aged 30. Like his 'sandgrown' father and grandfather before him, he earned a living from the bay by fishing with nets set from his horse and cart rather than by boat, so far out do the tides go. The experience gained from safely navigating the constantly changing topography helped him secure this ancient office. He led his first walk across Kent Sands in 1964, guiding paratroopers on military exercise, but has lost count of the tens of thousands of walkers he has guided, mostly in groups. Indeed, although he has never left the shores of the United Kingdom, in the 56 years he spent as The Queen's Guide to the Sands he was said to have walked the equivalent of twice around the world. He took Prince Philip across the sands by horse and carriage in 1985, but his services were never required by The Queen. ¶ If The Queen's Guide to the Sands could be said to have a symbol of office, it would be the long stick with which he tests the sand to find a safe path, every now and then pushing in a 'brob' of laurel grown on Guide's Farm, to act as a marker until the tide has covered it many times. He uses his eyes to assess the conditions, and daily witness of the elements has convinced him that our weather is indeed changing, with more rain, stronger winds and resulting higher tides. This dangerous combination means that The Queen's Guide to the Sands will continue to perform a vital life-saving function in guiding people across the dynamic tidal environment of Morecambe Bay.

Overleaf: Guiding stick in one hand, The Queen's Guide to the Sands holds 'brobs' of laurel in his other, which are placed at intervals to mark a safe route over the quixotic sands of Morecambe Bay.

QUEEN'S CHAMPION

The Manor of Scrivelsby Court in Lincolnshire has remained the home of the descendants of Robert Marmion since it was given to him by his friend William the Conqueror after the Battle of Hastings in 1066. From here, on the edge of the Lincolnshire Wolds, in order to fulfil the terms of William's grant, knights have ridden as Royal Champions into Coronation banquets at Westminster Hall, prepared to 'prove by his body, if need be, that the King is true and rightful heir to the kingdom'. ¶ Under Norman justice people could prove their innocence in trial by combat, by felling a fully armed knight without appropriate weaponry. The Dukes of Normandy employed specially selected knights to do combat on their behalf, especially to challenge anyone who cast doubt on their right to rule. Marmion had been one such knight in Normandy, and William offered him Scrivelsby on condition of accepting the role of King's Champion in his new kingdom. ¶ Generous privileges fell to the Champion, including 'the best but one' horse available from the royal stable; a fine saddle, armour and trappings for the horse; a complete suit of armour for the Champion, including a shield and lance; 20 yards of crimson satin; and the gold cup and cover with which the Sovereign drank his health at the banquet. ¶ The earliest record of the Champion ceremony at the Coronation of an English monarch dates from the accession of Richard II in 1377. The role had passed to Sir John Dymoke, who held the Manor of Scrivelsby in right of his wife Margaret, great-granddaughter of Philip Marmion, last Baron Marmion. ¶ The last occasion on which a Dymoke was called on to answer a challenge to the Sovereign was at the Coronation banquet of George IV in 1821. The Reverend John Dymoke held the title, but as a man of the cloth he was granted permission for his teenage son Henry to perform the duties. The doors of Westminster Hall were opened and Henry Dymoke, flanked by Great Officers of State, rode in to throw down his gauntlet. The Garter King of Arms read the challenge, which was repeated three times. ¶ No Coronation banquet was held for William IV, and it was decided not to include the Champion's ride and challenge at Victoria's Coronation, but at the accession of Edward VII the Champion was given the role of Standard Bearer of England instead. This tradition has continued and the then Queen's Champion, Lieutenant-Colonel John Dymoke, bore the Union Flag at the Coronation in 1953. Afterwards he wrote, 'Never again shall I see such regalia and a wondrous collection of fine jewellery. The banks must have been empty on the day.' ¶ The magnificent armour worn for the last time by the Champion and his horse at the Coronation of George IV is on display in St George's Hall at Windsor Castle. The Champion's armour was made at the royal workshops in Greenwich for Sir Christopher Hatton (1540–91), but in 1685 it appears to have been issued to the King's Champion, for use at the Coronation of James II.

Bridgeman Images

Above: 'Mr Dymoke, the King's Champion', from *An Authentic History of the Coronation of His Majesty King George the Fourth* by Robert Huish, 1821.
Overleaf: No descendant of Robert Marmion has ever been called to fight for his master. But when the challenge was made at George III's Coronation in 1761, silence fell: rumours abounded that Bonnie Prince Charlie was in London in order to do mortal combat with the Champion. The 35th Queen's Champion, and 34th Lord of the Manor of Scrivelsby, stands at the Lion Gateway to Scrivelsby Court holding the very glove thrown down in that challenge and the Union Flag borne by the Champion at Coronations.

QUEEN'S SCHOLARS

Every year academically gifted boys and girls take 'The Challenge', the exams that form part of the selection process for the next intake of Queen's Scholars at Westminster School in the religious and constitutional heart of London. Eight boys, aged 13, will be successful, and, since 2016, they have been joined by four 16-year-old girls who have sat subject-specific sixth form entrance exams. They join an illustrious roll call that includes Ben Jonson, John Locke, John Dryden and A.A. Milne. ¶ The Queen's Scholars become part of Elizabeth I's Royal Foundation of the College of St Peter which encompasses both Westminster School and Westminster Abbey. The school's origins date back to Henry VIII, however; following the dissolution of the monastery at Westminster Abbey in 1540 Henry established his new foundation, and in the 'Booke of the ereccion of the King's newe College', the charter states that 40 scholars are to be taught grammar. Today, the total number of Queen's Scholars is 48. Although the scholarships were established by Henry, they were more formally affirmed by Elizabeth I in 1560, whose charter states that 'the youth which is growing to manhood, as tender shoots in the wood of our state, shall be liberally instructed in good books to the greater honour of the state'. As a result of her confirmation of royal patronage, Elizabeth is celebrated as the school's foundress. ¶ Historic royal links are maintained by certain privileges granted to The Queen's Scholars: they may attend Parliamentary debates and special services in Westminster Abbey, which have included the 2010 visit of Pope Benedict XVI, the wedding of the Duke and Duchess of Cambridge in 2011 and the 60th anniversary of the Coronation. By ancient tradition, the Scholars attend Coronations and claim the right to acclaim the Sovereign with cries of 'Vivat Rex!' or 'Vivat Regina!' ¶ Regular duties for The Queen's Scholars include attending one Sunday Eucharist service in Westminster Abbey each term, singing Compline in the Abbey's St Faith's Chapel each Monday and participating in the school's annual Commemoration of Benefactors services. One of their daily duties is to guard the steps to School (the main hall) during Latin Prayers. Traditionally this role was to deter passers-by who might try to explore what was happening 'up School' (i.e. in the main hall).

The Queen's Scholars stand with their Master in the cloisters that link the school to Westminster Abbey. They wear the ecclesiastical-style surplice required for their attendance at Abbey services, while the scholar on the right wears the formal tail coat scholar's uniform.

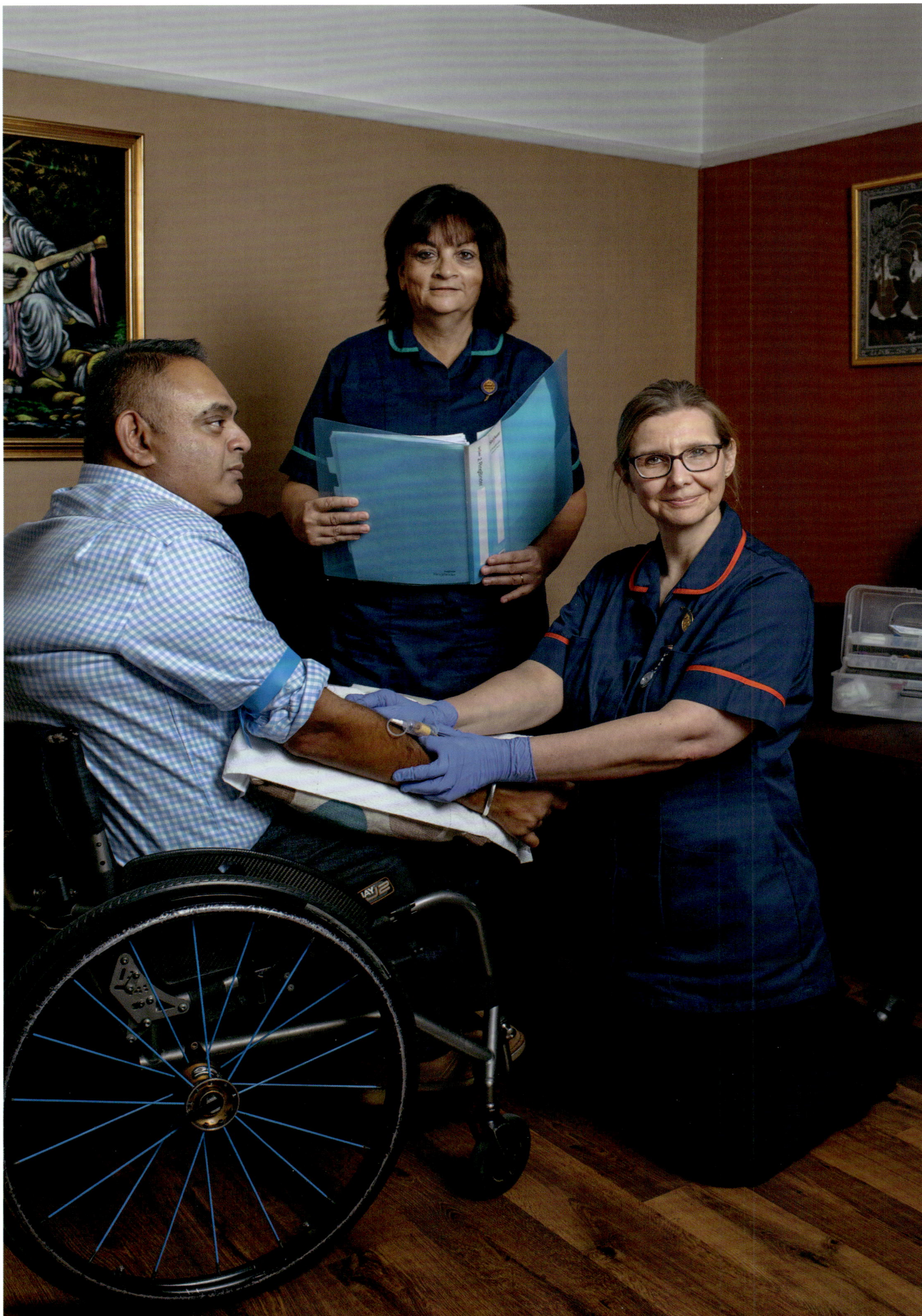

QUEEN'S NURSES

The title of Queen's Nurse has its origins in the district nursing movement that began in Liverpool in 1859. Philanthropist William Rathbone created the first district nursing scheme in the city and it soon spread to other parts of Britain and overseas. The first district nurses visited sick people in their own homes and brought the latest nursing techniques to people unable to pay for healthcare, almost a century before the creation of the National Health Service. ¶ It was Queen Victoria's Golden Jubilee of 1887 that provided district nursing with its greatest opportunity and legacy. A national collection was made by the women of the United Kingdom to honour Victoria, and after the purchase of some fabulous jewellery, there was a consensus that the remaining £70,000 should be used for philanthropic purposes. Rathbone drew up a plan for district nursing on a national basis, with the advice of Florence Nightingale. The Queen greatly admired Miss Nightingale, particularly since two Nightingale-trained nurses successfully treated her son Prince Alfred after an assassination attempt in Australia. She was therefore particularly pleased to give her royal assent to the plan. ¶ In 1889, a Royal Charter was issued for Queen Victoria's Jubilee Institute for Nurses (QVJIN), for 'the training, support and maintenance of women to act as nurses for the sick poor and ... the promotion and provision of improved means of nursing the sick poor'. The district nurses who were trained by the Institute were known as Queen's Nurses. ¶ Victoria, as the first Patron of the charity, took a

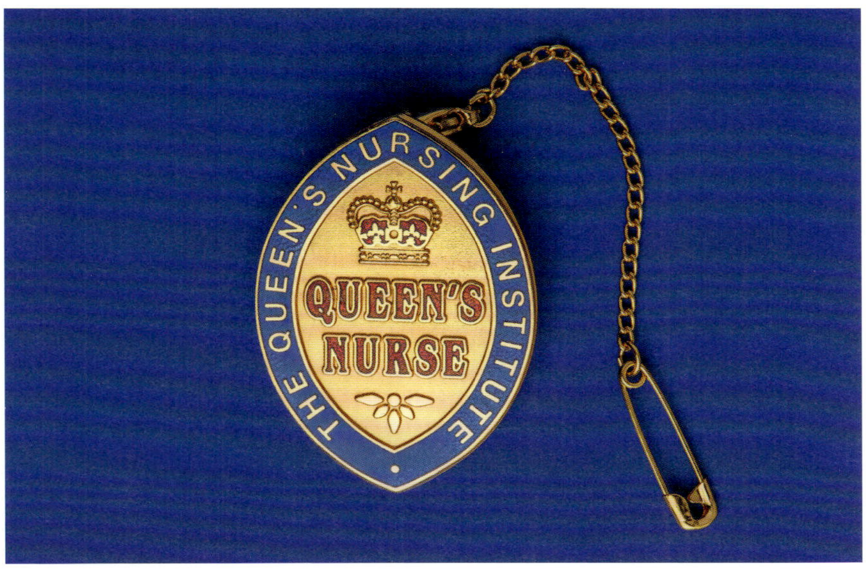

There are over 1,300 Queen's Nurses working in every part of England, Wales and Northern Ireland. As many nurses working in the community do not regularly wear a uniform, Queen's Nurses can be identified by The Queen's Nurse badge.

keen interest from the beginning and personally inspected the new Queen's Nurses at Windsor Castle in 1896 and on other occasions. This tradition was continued by the succeeding Patrons, Queen Alexandra, Queen Mary and Queen Elizabeth The Queen Mother. Her Majesty The Queen became the charity's Patron in 2002 and an annual gathering of Queen's Nurses is held at The Queen's garden at Frogmore, Windsor. ¶ The QVJIN was renamed The Queen's Institute of District Nursing in 1928 and The Queen's Nursing Institute (QNI) in 1973. Today the QNI operates in England, Wales and Northern Ireland and a separate branch of the charity, based in Edinburgh, operates in Scotland. The title of Queen's Nurse continued to be awarded to trained district nurses until 1968, when nurse education was absorbed into higher education and the title fell into abeyance for almost 40 years. In 2007, with the permission of The Queen, the QNI reintroduced the title as a professional development programme, followed by QNI Scotland in 2017. All nurses who work in the community, not just district nurses, are eligible to apply and there is a rigorous selection procedure. ¶ Today's Queen's Nurses can be nurses in any specialism in the community including general practice, learning disabilities, mental health, occupational health, school nursing and leaders in management and education. They deliver care to people in their own homes, in GP surgeries, in schools, in clinics and through street outreach work to homeless people and other vulnerable groups.

One of over 80 Queen's Nurses in Scotland visits one of her patients in rural Dumfries & Galloway. She wears the QNI Scotland badge bearing the Royal Cypher and thistle motif. The tartan was specially designed for The Queen's Nurses in Scotland.

NHS

PRESENTED BY HER MAJESTY QUEEN ELIZABETH II

FOR POETRY

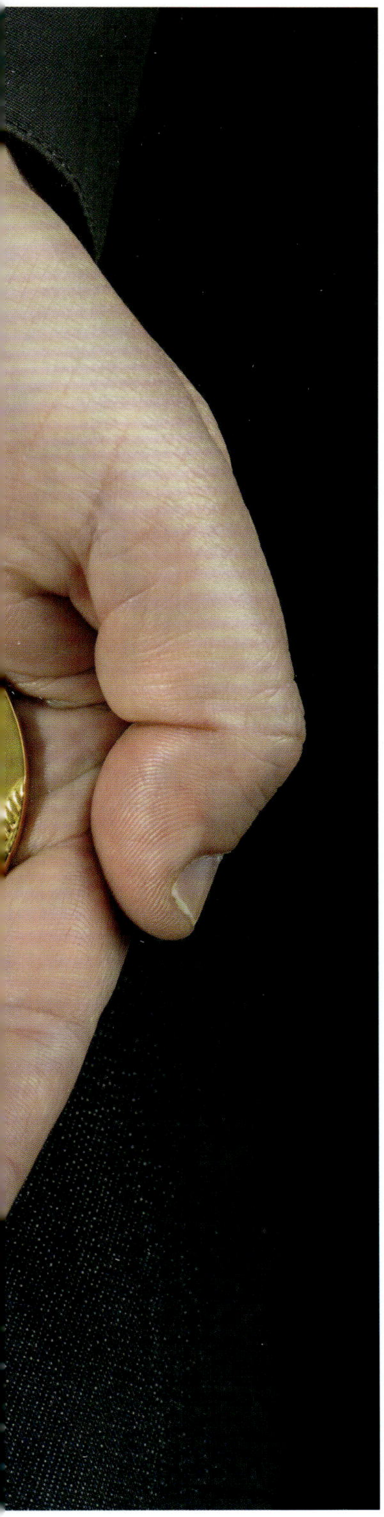

QUEEN'S GOLD MEDAL FOR POETRY AND POET LAUREATE

The English language has an ancient poetic tradition dating back to the works of anonymous Anglo-Saxon poets, such as the epic poem *Beowulf* and the surviving lines of *The Battle of Maldon*. Poets Geoffrey Chaucer and William Shakespeare enriched the language immeasurably, and both flourished under their Sovereigns. Chaucer spent his life at court as a diplomat and civil servant under Edward III, Richard II and Henry IV, while writing the *Canterbury Tales* and other foundational works of Middle English. A further link was forged between the monarch and poetic language when James I declared, upon succeeding to the throne after Queen Elizabeth's death in 1603, that he would be the new sponsor of Shakespeare's theatre company, which duly became the King's Men. ¶ A visible symbol of the value placed on poetic merit by the monarchy came in the form of the Gold Medal for Poetry instituted by King George V in 1933 at the suggestion of the then Poet Laureate John Masefield; the first medal was awarded to Lawrence Whistler the following year. It recognises excellence in poetry, judged either on a body of published work created over several years, or for an outstanding poetry collection issued during the year of the award. The poet must be from the United Kingdom or Commonwealth. ¶ The Queen's Poetry Medal Committee, which is always led by the current Poet Laureate, recommended Salford-born David Constantine as the 51st recipient in December 2020. ¶ The office of Poet Laureate, the highest honour in British poetry, has its roots in 1617 when playwright and poet Ben Jonson was granted a stipend by King James I for his literary services to the Crown. The post was not officially created, however, until 1668 when King Charles II issued letters patent to appoint John Dryden as Poet Laureate, although he was sacked in 1689 for refusing, as a

The reverse of The Queen's Gold Medal for Poetry (held here by Poet Laureate Simon Armitage) was designed by Edmund Dulac to represent Truth 'emerging from her well and holding in her right hand the divine flame of inspiration – Beauty is Truth and Truth Beauty'. The famous phrase is a quotation from John Keats's poem 'Ode on a Grecian Urn'. Dulac, born in France in 1882, moved to London in 1904 and became a naturalised British citizen. He was noted for his colour illustrations of high-quality editions of Shakespeare, classic literature and fairy tales, but after the First World War his career developed in new directions. He designed the commemorative postage stamp for the Coronation of King George V, and the head of the King used on all the stamps during his reign was Dulac's creation. One of the stamps of the set issued to commemorate the Coronation of Queen Elizabeth II was also his design, but he died just before it was issued, in May 1953.

Catholic, to swear allegiance to William and Mary. Since then a further 20 poets have been chosen in recognition of their work of national significance, with only one woman to be honoured to date – Carol-Ann Duffy, who held the post from 2009 to 2019. ¶ Poet Laureates, who have included Wordsworth, Tennyson, Sir John Betjeman and Ted Hughes, initially served until their death before a fixed term of ten years was introduced in 1999, when the role was given to Andrew Motion. The position is honorary and the individual poet is now free to decide whether or not to produce poetry for national occasions or royal events. Current Poet Laureate Simon Armitage says that he finds it stimulating to write such commissioned poems, as they often have to include modern terms and technical words. Since taking on the role in 2019, he has written verse marking events as diverse as the 50th anniversary of the first moon landing, the centenary of the burial of the Unknown Warrior in Westminster Abbey and the Covid-19 lockdown. The Poet Laureate takes home an annual stipend of £5,750, along with the traditional 'butt of sack', namely some 720 bottles of sherry. Since 1984, when Ted Hughes took on the role, the sherry has been a gift from the sherry producers of Spain to celebrate the cultural and trading links between Britain and Spain. The Poet Laureate is invited to Jerez to select from a wide variety; Armitage chose Fino, Amontillado and Cream sherries. ¶ Today's Poet Laureate is selected from a shortlist drawn up by an advisory panel of people immersed in the fields of poetry, literature and the arts. The Culture Secretary and the Prime Minister make their choice to be put forward to The Queen for approval, before a public announcement is made.

The Poet Laureate holds The Queen's Gold Medal for Poetry in front of his poem 'Snow' carved into blocks of gritstone in an old quarry near Marsden, West Yorkshire, where he was born and raised. The poem is one of six he composed for the Ilkley Literature Festival in 2010, responding to the landscape of the Pennine Watershed. The poems, each describing water in a different form, are carved into the rock along a stretch of 47 miles. While the Pennine rocks and crags provided an elemental playground during his boyhood, words are now the Poet Laureate's raw material from which he hews his poems. He writes in longhand in a notebook, drafting and redrafting, until a poem is ready to move into print; seeing the poem in the livery of text prompts another phase of revision. Writing by hand is necessary to slow the hand to something closer to the speed of poetic composition. He likens the manual act of writing to sculpting and carving words, in keeping with the idea of craft. It takes time, but as expressed in the last line of his poem 'Lockdown', 'the journey a ponderous one at times, long and slow / but necessarily so'.

THE
QUEEN'S
GALLANTRY
MEDAL

QUEEN'S GALLANTRY MEDAL

The Queen's Gallantry Medal is the United Kingdom's third highest award for bravery, after the George Cross and the George Medal. Instituted in 1974, it replaced the Order of the British Empire for Gallantry and the British Empire Medal for Gallantry. ¶ As of December 2019, 548 civilians and 542 military personnel have had their 'exemplary acts of bravery' recognised by receipt of this silver medal. Three posthumous awards announced in 2018 and 2019 bring the total number of posthumous recipients to 41. The most recent posthumous award was given to Andrew Foster, who died in 2017 saving the life of his wife in a major rockfall in Yosemite National Park, California. ¶ The award to Leading Seaman (Seaman Specialist) Sally Louise Hughes makes her the 25th female recipient. Leading Seaman Hughes saved 14 sailors after their yacht lost its mast in rough seas 500 miles off Land's End. She made 13 trips in a RIB from HMS *Dragon* until the entire crew was safely aboard her Type 45 Destroyer. ¶ In 2017, a replacement medal was presented to Margaret Warby QGM, on the 40th anniversary of the Granville railway disaster in Sydney, Australia. Eighty-four people, including an unborn baby, died when a crowded commuter train derailed. Margaret was one of six rescuers who earned Queen's Gallantry Medals, but her original medal was stolen. ¶ If the anonymity of a medal recipient must be preserved for operational reasons, The Queen presents the award in a private ceremony in an antechamber before the main investiture ceremony.

The silver Queen's Gallantry Medal, shown here on the reverse side, is 36mm in diameter. The obverse bears The Queen's effigy, and the recipient's name is engraved on the rim. If a recipient is granted a further award of the medal, their achievement is indicated by a silver bar ornamented with laurel leaves worn on the ribbon.

QUEEN'S FIRE SERVICE MEDAL

The dedication and bravery of the Fire and Rescue Service was fully recognised in 1954 by the establishment of The Queen's Fire Service Medal. Since 1909, when Edward VII instituted the King's Police Medal, firemen had been eligible for this award alongside police officers in Britain and the Empire. The name changed in 1940 to the King's Police and Fire Services Medal to reflect its dual nature, but with the separation of The Queen's Fire Service Medal and The Queen's Police Medal in 1954, the specific challenges faced by the Fire and Rescue Service were finally given their due. ¶ The Royal Warrant of 4 June 1954 declared that the medal be awarded to those members of a fire brigade who have 'either performed acts of exceptional courage and skill at the cost of their lives, or exhibited conspicuous devotion to duty'. The award has two categories, the most common being for Distinguished Service. The equivalent award for Gallantry can only be granted posthumously and has, up to 2020, never been awarded. Fire and Rescue Service members are also eligible for the George Cross, George Medal and The Queen's Gallantry Medal.

Eighteen years after first joining the Fire and Rescue Service, Rebecca Bryant was awarded The Queen's Fire Service Medal in 2020 in recognition of her distinguished service. Since 2016, she has been Chief Fire Officer (CFO)/Chief Executive with Staffordshire Fire and Rescue Service and is the first woman CFO to have progressed through the ranks in the UK, not just England.

QUEEN'S POLICE MEDAL

In January 1909 Edwardian London was transfixed by an armed robbery in Tottenham that, over a six-mile chase, cost two lives and 23 casualties, during which 400 rounds of ammunition were fired by the two thieves. One of the dead and seven of the injured were policemen. In recognition of the bravery shown by the police, none of whom were armed save for a few pistols borrowed from members of the public, seven months later Edward VII instituted the King's Police Medal for a police officer who has 'performed acts of exceptional courage and skill or exhibited conspicuous devotion to duty'. Several of the policemen involved in the 'Tottenham Outrage' were among the first recipients in November 1909. ¶ The original Royal Warrant for the medal included members of fire brigades, both at home and within British Dominions and Territories, as eligible for the award. To reflect their inclusion, the medal was renamed the King's Police and Fire Services Medal in 1940, but in 1954 it was again renamed The Queen's Police Medal when The Queen's Fire Service Medal was also instituted. ¶ The most common form of the current award is The Queen's Police Medal for Distinguished Service. The Queen's Police Medal for Gallantry can only be awarded posthumously, and was last awarded in 1976 to the late PC Stephen Tibble, who was killed in February 1975 while off duty. The 21-year-old Metropolitan Police officer saw colleagues chasing a man and went to assist on his motorbike, but the suspect, a member of the IRA, fatally shot him three times in the chest. Acts of police gallantry are usually now recognised with the George Cross, George Medal, The Queen's Gallantry Medal or The Queen's Commendation for Bravery. ¶ In one of her final actions as Home Secretary, in 2016 Theresa May recommended that more officers of junior ranks should receive The Queen's Police Medal, to recognise their vital role in protecting the public at a community level. In the 2017 New Year's Honours over half of the 17 recipients of the award were officers below the rank of superintendent.

The Queen's Police Medal is made of silver with The Queen's head on the obverse, and on the reverse a design emblematic of protection from danger. The name of the person to whom the medal is awarded is engraved on the rim. PC Thomas Farrell (top right) of the Suffolk Constabulary was awarded The Queen's Police Medal in 2020 for his work investigating the online sexual abuse of children and his development of technology to tackle such abuse. Sergeant Mohammed Najib (bottom right) of the West Midlands Police was awarded The Queen's Police Medal in 2020 to recognise his work with Birmingham's mosques to divert vulnerable people from radicalisation. He founded the Birmingham Council of Mosques, which shares anti-radicalisation messages in the Muslim communities and provides sports and social projects for young people.

SUFFOLK
CONSTABULARY
FORCE HEADQUARTERS
MARTLESHAM HEATH

LOBB
LONDON

QUEEN ELIZABETH SCHOLARSHIP TRUST SCHOLARS AND APPRENTICES

The unseen hands of craftspeople are evident in many of the portraits in this book – embroiderers, saddlers, jewellers, tailors, instrument makers and goldsmiths continue ancient traditions of skilled making that have enriched the nation's State Ceremonial and historic offices. ¶ Many of these talented individuals have been beneficiaries of The Queen Elizabeth Scholarship Trust (QEST), founded by the Royal Warrant Holders Association in 1990 to celebrate the 150th anniversary of the Association and the 90th birthday of Queen Elizabeth The Queen Mother. The charity supports excellence in British craftsmanship and offers scholarship and apprenticeship funding to gifted makers working across the full spectrum of crafts, from traditional to contemporary, and from every corner of the British Isles. Many QEST scholars have gone on to become leaders in their field, such as renowned potter Julian Stair, and two-thirds are currently teaching, passing on their skills and ensuring a thriving future for British craft. ¶ Applications for funding are open to all talented and aspiring makers living in the UK. Successful applicants receive funding to further their training and develop their skills through a college course, graduate degree, vocational training or one-to-one learning with a master craftsperson. Previous scholars include artists who studied drawing and painting at the Charles H. Cecil Studios in Florence, glassblowers who spent time at the Pilchuck Glass School in Washington State and a tapestry weaver who learnt kasuri weaving in Japan. Apprentice funding supports the training of craftspeople at an earlier stage in their career, and examples include a scenic artist at the National Theatre and a glass blower at Dartington Crystal. ¶ Scholars and apprentices receive additional support from QEST with business skills seminars, promotion and opportunities to collaborate and exhibit their work. Previous scholars have worked on a number of prestigious commissions such as The Queen's summer house at Buckingham Palace, while students on the Traditional Building Skills programme, run in collaboration with The Prince's Foundation, completed work on a walled garden pavilion at Hillsborough Castle in Northern Ireland.

Queen Elizabeth Scholarship Trust Scholars and Apprentices are drawn from many disciplines and all parts of the UK. Featured here are a decorative artist from Sussex, a sculptor from York, a bespoke tailor and an apprentice boot- and shoemaker from London, a farrier from Devon and a gold- and silversmith from the Shetland Isles.

KING'S TROOP, ROYAL HORSE ARTILLERY

This book concludes with an anomaly. While the offices featured here bear 'Queen's' in their name as long as the reign of Queen Elizabeth II endures, The King's Troop, Royal Horse Artillery will always retain 'King's' in its title regardless of the gender of the Sovereign. This break with precedent dates to 1946 and the creation of the Riding Troop by King George VI. ¶ The King decided that, following the mechanisation of the last batteries of horse-drawn artillery, a troop of horse artillery should be kept to take part in the great ceremonies of State, such as the firing of Royal Salutes in Hyde Park. On 17 April 1946, therefore, the Riding Troop was formed as the saluting battery of the Household Troops. When the King visited the Troop at its St John's Wood Barracks on 24 October 1947, he crossed out 'Riding' and wrote 'King's' when he signed the visitors' book. The Queen, as Captain-General of the Royal Artillery, chose not to change the name to 'Queen's Troop' out of respect for her father. ¶ It was the outbreak of war with revolutionary France that prompted the formation of Britain's first two Troops of horse artillery in 1793 to provide mobile fire support for the cavalry. This gives the Royal Horse Artillery (RHA) the highest precedence in the British Army, even above its parent unit the Royal Artillery, with only The Life Guards and The Blues and Royals ranking above it. ¶ The development of the 'galloper' or 'grasshopper' gun had meant that a gun could be pulled by one horse between the shafts, so guns could now keep pace with fast-moving troops. During Wellington's Peninsular campaign of 1810–13 the reputation of the RHA was firmly established. In 1899 the Royal Artillery was split into two, with the RHA joining the Royal Field Artillery as part of the first group. This arrangement lasted throughout the First World War, which could be called 'the Gunner's War', so central was the role of artillery on both sides. The six Quick Firing 13-pounder guns of today's King's Troop were part of the Army's huge firepower on the Western Front. In 1924 the two groups were reamalgamated into the Royal Artillery. With horses no longer weapons of war, the RHA's batteries served with armoured troops and other artillery units during the Second World War. ¶ In addition to firing Royal Salutes and providing a gun carriage and a team of black horses for State and military funerals, King's Troop soldiers also mount The Queen's Life Guard at Horse Guards each summer when the Household Cavalry Mounted Regiment is on military training outside London. The King's Troop, known as the 'Gunners', has a vital operational role too. Its soldiers are trained as a fighting force, and when the Army mobilises, the unit provides heavy goods vehicle drivers who deliver ammunition to artillery units on the battlefield. ¶ The Troop's 130 Irish Draught horses range in colour from the light

bays of 'A' Sub section to the cavalry blacks of 'F' Sub section, which pull the gun carriage for State funerals. They last performed this duty for the funeral of Baroness Thatcher in 2013. When the Troop provided the gun carriage for the ceremony of the interment of the Unknown Soldier at Westminster Abbey on 11 November 1920, some of the cavalry blacks had seen action in the First World War.

At the former King's Troop barracks at St John's Wood, just before the Troop moved to Woolwich Garrison, The Queen signs her name to reassert that there will always be a King's Troop, regardless of whether there is a King or a Queen on the throne. The special bond between the monarch and The King's Troop continues, cemented by their shared affection for horses.

In 2017, to mark the 70th anniversary of the formation of The King's Troop, a Royal Review was held in Hyde Park. Afterwards The Queen met King's Troop soldiers and veterans, including Percy Austen who was serving when George VI inspected the Parade in 1947, and the first female Master Saddler and Master Tailor. Uniquely for the British Army, this Troop is currently 50/50 male and female. The Queen was also reintroduced to her former racehorse Knock Castle, who was in training to become one of the Gunner horses.

Queen's Consort
Prince Philip, The Duke of Edinburgh

Queen's Heirs
Prince George
Prince Charles, the Prince of Wales
Prince William, the Duke of Cambridge

Queen's Dresser
Angela Kelly

Queen's Pages of the Backstairs
Left to right:
Barry Mitford
Paul Whybrew

Queen's Stud Groom
Terry Pendry

Queen's Equerries
Left to right:
Captain Jonny Olley, Coldstream Guards
Lieutenant-Colonel Charles Richards, Welsh Guards
Lieutenant-Colonel Nana Kofi Twumasi-Ankrah, Household Cavalry

Queen's Piper
Pipe Major Scott Methven, Argyll & Sutherland Highlanders

Queen's Body Guard of the Honourable Corps of Gentlemen-at-Arms
Left to right:
Lieutenant-Colonel Rory Ingleby-MacKenzie
Lieutenant-Colonel John Kaye, Clerk of the Cheque and Adjutant
Major Charles Macfarlane, Harbinger
The Right Honourable the Lord Taylor of Holbeach, Captain
Major Rupert Lendrum
Major David Kennard, Standard Bearer
Colonel Ewen Cameron
Colonel Christopher MacKenzie-Beevor, Lieutenant

Queen's Body Guard of the Yeomen of the Guard
Left to right:
Messenger Sergeant Major Chris Savage (late Grenadier Guards)
Divisional Sergeant Major Michael Dabbs (late Grenadier Guards)
Divisional Sergeant Major William Tuffs (late Coldstream Guards)
Yeoman Bed Goer Keith Robinson (late Coldstream Guards)
Yeoman Bed Goer Peter Fairnie (late Irish Guards)
Colonel Michael Kingscote, Lieutenant
Yeoman Colin Coull (late Scots Guards)
Yeoman Ken Moffat (Royal Engineers)

Queen's Apothecary
Dr Tim Evans

Surveyor of The Queen's Pictures
Desmond Shawe-Taylor

Surveyor of The Queen's Works of Art
Rufus Bird

Queen's Gurkha Orderly Officer
Captain (Major) Buddhi Bahadur Bhandiari
Captain Mukti Prasad Gurung

Queen's Flag Sergeant
Sergeant Nathan Bowen

Queen's Pages of Honour
Lachlan Legge-Bourke (Lochy)
The Honourable Augustus Stanhope (Gus)
Master Thomas Hallé
The Marquis of Lorne (Archie)

Queen's Page of Honour in Scotland
The Honourable Augustus Stanhope (Gus)

Queen's Archers
Left to right:
C J A Bewsher
Lieutenant-Colonel J C Stewart, Adjutant
His Grace the Duke of Buccleuch and Queensbury, Captain-General
W R Simpson, Match Secretary
Lieutenant-Colonel R Callander, Secretary

Queen's Bloodstock Adviser, Queen's Racehorse Trainer and Queen's Racing Colours
Left to right:
John Warren
Sir Michael Stoute
Ryan Moore

Queen's Lofts Manager
Peter Farrow

Queen's Company Grenadier Guards
Members of The Queen's Company Grenadier Guards

Queen's Long Guard
Members of the Household Cavalry Mounted Regiment

Household Cavalry State Trumpeter
LCpl of Horse Kate Sandford

Queen's Guard
Formed by the Coldstream Guards, led by Captain Thomas Tollemache

Queen's Flight and Queen's Colour Squadron
Members of the Queen's Flight and Queen's Colour Squadron

Queen's Bargemaster
Left to right:
Paul Ludwig
Robert Prentice, Fishmongers' Company Bargemaster

Queen's Swan Marker
David Barber

Queen's Chaplains
Paul Wright, Deputy Clerk
Rupert Charkham
Peter Holliday
David Nicholson
Jeremy Haselock
Nicholas Thistlethwaite
Rose Hudson-Wilkin
Hugh Bearn
Paul Miller
Kevan McCormack
Edward Lewis
Ian Davenport
Rt Rev James Newcome, Bishop of Carlisle and Clerk of the Closet

Queen's Almsmen
Left to right:
Albert Gordon
Harold Hall
Mike Dyer
Alex McBride

Mariama Ifode-Blease
John Bassett

Queen's Harbour Master
David Lightfoot

Queen's Messenger
Jake Clark
Barry Daniels (Driver)

Queen's Remembrancer
Honourable Ms Justice Barbara Fontaine
James Chapman, Beadle of Goldsmiths' Company
Timothy Schroder, Prime Warden of Goldsmiths' Company

Queen's Counsel
Left to right:
Paul Garlick QC
Kieron Beal QC
Gemma White QC
Catrin Evans QC
Nicholas Vineall QC
Richard Spearman QC
Martin Forde QC
Mark Trafford QC
Alison Foster QC
Rosina Cottage QC
Adrienne Page QC
David Price QC (Solicitor Advocate)
Robert Seabrook QC
Nicholas Lavender QC
Jack Button, barristers' clerk
Georgina Gills, barristers' clerk

Queen's Scouts
Centre: Peter Moody, Hampshire Scouts Vice President, with Vicky.
Lizzie Harvey, Liam Holden, Greg Humphrey, Rhia Wilton, Keith Edwards, Victoria Edwards, Martina Dickison

Queen's Guide to the Sands
Cedric Robinson

Queen's Champion
Francis Dymoke

Queen's Scholars
Mark Feltham, Master of The Queen's Scholars

Queen's Nurses
Helen Mehra
Lesley Broad (kneeling)
Patient – Indeep Sidhu

Queen's Nurse in Scotland
Hazel Hamilton

Queen's Gold Poetry Medal and Poet Laureate
Simon Armitage

Queen's Fire Service Medal
Chief Fire Officer Rebecca Bryant

Queen's Police Medal
Top: Police Constable Tom Farrell
Bottom: Sergeant Najib Mohammed

Queen Elizabeth Scholarship Trust Scholars & Apprentices
Clockwise from top left:
Melissa White, decorative artist
Andrian Melka, sculptor
Jennie Adamson, bespoke tailor
Olu Fadairo, apprentice boot- and shoemaker
Nina Thomas, farrier
Rod Kelly, gold- and silversmith

King's Troop Royal Horse Artillery
Lieutenant-Colonel Neil Cross
Major General Matthew Sykes

ACKNOWLEDGEMENTS

Buckingham Palace:
Vice Admiral Sir Tony Johnstone-Burt; Lieutenant-Colonel Michael Vernon; Donal McCabe; Hannah Howard
Sarah Davis – Royal Collection

Household Division:
Major-General Christopher Ghika – Officer Commanding Household Division; Lieutenant-Colonel Guy Stone – Brigade Major; Susan Coulthard – Army Communications HQ London District; Lieutenant-Colonel Neil Cross RA

Central Chancery of the Orders of Knighthood:
Lieutenant-Colonel Stephen Segrave

Queen Elizabeth Scholarship Trust:
Deborah Pocock; Katherine Boyle

Yeoman Usher Brigadier Neil Baverstock

Robert Crouch, Past Bargemaster

Stephen Connelly, Cleave & Company

Adrienne Page QC; Ian Mayes QC

My thanks to Minna Rossi, my assistant on most of the portraits, and to Robert Chadwick; Prof. Phil Cleaver of *et al design consultants* who designed the book, assisted by Jennifer Penny; Joe Thomas who prepared the pictures for print. I am so grateful to Tamsin Shelton, who wrote, compiled and edited the text, for her enthusiasm for this book. My thanks to friends Alastair Bruce for his Foreword and David Yarrow whose generosity made the production of this book possible.

A portrait of King George IV by Sir Thomas Lawrence RA being hung for the exhibition *George IV: Art & Spectacle* in The Queen's Gallery, Buckingham Palace, in 2019. Commissioned in 1821, the painting depicts the King in the luxuriant costume he designed for his Coronation, and wearing collars of the Golden Fleece, Guelphic, Bath and Garter chivalric orders. The 16-foot silk velvet and ermine robe reflects George's love of extravagant fashion, to satisfy which he incurred debts all his life. Indeed, his Coronation was the most expensive in the history of the British monarchy, costing £238,000, roughly equivalent to £14 million today. The portrait still hangs in its original location in the Throne Room at St James's Palace, between *The Battle of Vittoria* and *The Battle of Waterloo* (both 1822) by George Jones. Lawrence was the leading British portraitist of the early 1800s, whose flattering and grandiose style appealed to royalty and the aristocracy. Largely self-taught, he became Painter-in-Ordinary to George III upon the death of Joshua Reynolds in 1792, and in 1794 was admitted as a full member of the Royal Academy. He rose to be President of the RA in 1820.

A CIP catalogue record for this book is available from the British Library

ISBN 978-0-9553253-9-7

Designed and typeset by Prof. Phil Cleaver
and Jennifer Penny of
et al design consultants (www.etal-design.com)
Typeset in Monotype Bembo Book
Print production and management by dlm creative,
(www.dlm-creative.com)
Printed on 170gsm Galerie Art Satin

Edited by Tamsin Shelton
Picture preparation by Joe Thomas (www.joe-digital.com)